MEMOIRS OF A CITIZEN-POLITICIAN

AN IDEALISTIC JOURNEY IN

STATE LEGISLATIVE POLITICS

By Dr. LeRoy D. Owens

2nd Edition

Updated by David L. Owens

DEDICATION

To all those who make American representative politics as good as it is: candidates, the elected officials, and mostly to the spouses, families, and campaign workers, for better government through the elective process.

Legal Notes

Second Edition

Copyright © 2021 David L. Owens

First Edition
Copyright © 1984 Dr. LeRoy Owens

David Owens

Owens@ipacific.com

TABLE OF CONTENTS

Introduction — 6

1. Becoming a Politician — 8
2. Organizing a Campaign — 11
3. Campaign Strategy — 19
4. Throwing my Hat into the Ring — 25
5. Getting Endorsed — 27
6. Volunteer Campaigning — 29
7. Citizen Participation Committee — 31
8. "Call LeRoy" — 34
9. The Bus — 37
10. Speaking to the Issues — 44
11. Track Coach Politics — 45
12. Town Meeting Politics — 53
13. Election Night Fever — 60
14. Serving as a Legislator — 63
15. Learning the Legislative Process — 69
16. The Camp Adair "Giveaway" — 73
17. A State "Jobs" Program — 86
18. A Weighted-Vote Plan for Apportionment — 89
19. The "Humanitarian Award" — 95
20. A Bill for Hitchers, Hikers, and Bikers — 101
21. A Proposal for Fair Qualifications for Employment — 104
22. After the Session and before the Next Election — 108
23. Public Ownership of Land — 112
24. Legal Concept of "Original Responsibility" — 118
25. Citizen Politics Now and Later — 121

INTRODUCTION

I guess I always wanted to be a politician. Like other kids who were born in the middle 1930s and experienced the migration of farm folks from the Middle West to states farther west, I grew up with the feeling that people made their own opportunities. I knew no particular deprivation as a child, though, looking back, my family "lived through" the somewhat despondent and financially uncertain years of national depression surviving day to day.

Like other children of those times, I can recall numerous incidents that demonstrated the difficulties my parents faced in raising five children with no continuous or adequate means of financial support. However, I have no recollection of ever having been slighted by this experience or ever consciously feeling any indignity for being what others might call poor.

And at no time can I recall associating the economic condition of the country with political factors. We seemed to accept what we were and the circumstances of day-to-day economic survival, blaming no one but ourselves for our family condition.

Politics was far removed from the practicality of daily living.

I cannot recall ever having any feeling except admiration and wonderment for people who were called the "mayor," the "congressman," or the "governor." I grew up with only respect for those who were elected by the people to serve them.

Becoming a politician was, to me, like becoming a minister, a missionary, a teacher, or a doctor. These people were special and deserved the support of other more ordinary folks because of the special responsibility they exercised. To this day, I maintain a fervent empathy for such people and am proud that I was "called upon" to serve in such company.

This book is intended to relate anecdotes that document happenings in my own experience in emerging from ordinary citizen status to a position in the Oregon state legislature, in the hope that others might better understand the nature of American citizen politics.

I hope that others, in reading this collection of stories and impressions, will acquire and share, (if they don't already), my admiration and respect for those who are elected to serve the rest of us.

Chapter 1
Becoming a Politician

As I grew up, my parents and teachers impressed upon me the same simple notion: "Anyone can be president." I enjoyed reading stories about George Washington and Abraham Lincoln, who began as insignificant ragamuffins and somehow, through the power of personal dedication and magnetism, willed and worked their way to ultimate levels of human destiny.

No station in life seemed higher to me than being elected to serve. I do not know to what extent this perception was based on conditioned patriotism, a personal need for acceptance, or childlike idealism. I just know that I held this strong feeling and dreamed that I might someday become the kind of person that would fit that idealistic model.

Early in the 1970s, I decided to run for a seat in the Oregon State House of Representatives. From a practical viewpoint, I suppose I had no business seeking a political office that paid a salary of $250 a month, plus daily expenses. Oregon was proud of its tradition of citizen legislative representation, which usually meant that those elected could afford to serve, often because they were well-to-do farmers with slack time in the winter anyway or lawyers with career or client interests to motivate them.

Altruistic, idealistic, would-be citizen legislators usually self-selected themselves away from running for office because of family financial necessity. I recall a close friend remarking to me, "If you can't support your family, you have no business running for office." Sometimes, ambitious would-be U.S. senators and governors ran for Oregon political offices with the backing of well-to-do families, or, too often, employers who saw advantage in a "friendly" vote in a legislative seat.

It was not unusual for other citizen legislators to be former lobbyists who had been paid advocates for sizable business or financial interests in the state. Few educators ran for political office because the nature of their employment made release from their jobs practically impossible.

Just a few years previous to my decision to run, a fellow educator had been fired up on his election to the legislature and went to court to require his employer to give him a leave of absence for the duration of the legislative session. In my case, I was not a regularly employed teacher and was working on a state-funded program to train older citizens for self-advocacy.

I had little reason to suspect that the program that I directed would be denied continued funding in the middle of the primary campaign. Friends more astute with the application of practical politics to such matters warned me that a program under the administration of the Republican governor would not be likely to continue to fund a program under the direction of an upstart Democratic party candidate. I had carefully discussed the financial implications of my serving in the legislature (should I be elected), with a Republican friend whose seat in the legislature I was seeking to hold (he had chosen not to run for re-election).

Having found that my wife could be hired as my secretary at a salary of $650 a month, and that I would receive $25 a day for expenses in addition to the legislative salary of $250 a month, my wife and I determined that we could just about maintain the needed family income, including rental on a second home in Salem (Oregon's capital city) and the additional expenses of becoming a legislator's family.

Besides finances, we discussed what running for office would mean to school schedules and family life in general. Of course, none of us really knew what we were getting into, but all agreed that if I thought it important to run, the family was certainly behind me.

I was to find, however, that deciding to run was only one of several beginning steps in a decision to seek public office.

Chapter 2
Organizing a Campaign

Actually, my decision to seek election to the Oregon House of Representatives came as a result of a variety of experiences relating to efforts to improve the lot of several groups of people with whom I had worked in previous years. The plight of older people and the failing condition of our educational institutions to serve the needs of children, were both motivating factors in my determination to seek a position of increased influence for making changes.

I supposed I would have considerable support from the constituencies with whom I had worked, notably with schoolteachers, the parents of schoolchildren, older citizens, and other persons I had known in various community and professional endeavors.

My reasons for wishing to seek public office were positive, I felt. I wanted to touch the conscience and perhaps the latent dedication of others who might join with me to represent their interests in the state legislature. In other words, I suspected that a coalition of individuals around issues and ideas generally relating to improvement of the human condition could form a basis of support for a practically unknown, but potentially electable, candidate.

I saw the necessity appealing to the imagination and idealistic desire I felt that most people possessed for challenging the inequities of our society and promoting betterment through the election of persons who closely represented their own altruism. Behind this notion was a psychological theory that I had studied and applied openly as a teacher trainer and as a change agent (self-appointed) in several situations.

This idea is technically known as "Festinger's Theory of Cognitive Dissonance." I had utilized this idea for a long time and had been delighted to discover such an erudite description for a change process that I had observed and used without realizing its technical sophistication. This theory postulates that if people are not happy with a current state of affairs (are dissonant), their frustration will drive them to change the present circumstance or rationalize why things must stay the way they are.

This idea further suggests that if people recognize that things are not the way they would like them to be and are presented with a practical and logical way to bring about needed changes, and if they are shown how these changes can be implemented (and afforded), the people will support the proposed change as well as the politician who makes such logical sense.

Further, if the politician appears to be truly dedicated and demonstrates this dedication through personal action and possesses an identity as a common and trustworthy person, he or she can expect support. If enough citizens can be induced to participate in a campaign to bring about such changes, they can share participatory success in the election of their candidate.

Having made the decision to run, I realized that I could not expect to win the election without a great deal of volunteer help. I had had considerable experience in organizing community causes but knew little about the intricacies and pitfalls of financing, and implementing, a potentially successful campaign. I knew that I must find the best management help and that I had no money with which to buy expertise.

I somehow knew that money wasn't the prime ingredient for organizing a dedicated and effective political organization, but I knew also that a considerable amount of money would be needed to purchase newspaper and other media advertising, as well as to purchase other political trivia needed to gain name familiarity with the voters. I felt that my best approach would be to appeal to the mutual interests of the best potential campaign leadership my political party could offer.

After a few telephone calls, I learned that several key people held the respect and possessed the inventive brain power I needed to mount a low-budget campaign and utilize a large cadre of volunteer workers.

My first task would be to generate enthusiasm among those whom I hoped would help manage the campaign, and to stir enthusiasm for my own candidacy from the party ranks of faithful Democratic party members who could energetically back a heavy issue-oriented campaign. I felt that I could generate volunteer assistance from a wide range of citizens who had little political experience, but who would be willing to help elect someone they felt would represent their interests in the state legislature.

My next task, then, was to appeal to the best potential campaign management in the local Democratic party organization. If I could gain the confidence of such dedicated campaign leadership, I felt that potential success of a volunteer citizen committee would be possible.

I was able to ascertain who the most respected managers of past campaigns had been and those most likely to be enthusiastic about my particular philosophy and campaign strategy. I possessed a high level of idealism and felt that if I was going to put the enormous amount of effort I intended into the campaign, it was essential that those working with me share my issue orientation and my dedication to societal change. It was essential that my campaign staff agree with me about issues and thus be enthusiastic about my potential as a state representative. Besides a common perspective on issues, I felt that both my campaign organization and I must share a dedication to interpersonal respect based upon honesty, openness, and enthusiasm.

My first telephone contact to potential campaign supporters was met with guarded optimism and an invitation to come right over and talk further. This first contact was a couple I had already considered to be friends, and whom I respected as dedicated and issue-oriented party regulars. I had not been active in Democratic party organization up to this time, and I felt I needed the advice of persons I respected to give me their opinion on my potential as a candidate and the style of campaigning I should insist upon.

When this couple met me at the door of their gracious home, I immediately felt at ease with their judgment. The unpretentiousness of their surroundings and the feeling that what happened to people was more important than living-room décor, made me at ease. These friends had both been active in community efforts that I identified as humanistic and environmentally conscious. I felt I could trust their judgment to help me to decide whether to continue or to abort my political and campaign interests.

After a few minutes of discussion, I found my own enthusiasm being reinforced and the idealism I felt warmed by two people who had spent years at helping others in the interest of better government and representative democracy. They were not a wealthy couple but shared the wealth of information and dedication that could only have been gained through years of sensitive and respectful participation in a political process in which neither had sought glory or aggrandizement.

These fine people encouraged me to continue my endeavor to organize a strong campaign committee and recommended that I talk to another politically active couple who were, in their judgment, among the strongest of past party leaders, as well as those best experienced in practicable campaign strategy. They also assured me that they were people I would like and would be apt to relate to as personal friends.

 Finally, they agreed to serve on campaign committees, should I pursue the effort seriously. This initial meeting produced in me almost a reverence for the dedication and commitment these people had exhibited over the years to better their community and state through their participation in citizen politics.

I approached my next visit with some trepidation. The male counterpart of the couple was a former president of the Lane County Democratic party, was a renowned political-science professor, and had years of political experience in various states prior to choosing to live in the Willamette Valley of Oregon. His brilliant wife had been described to me as the most effective campaign manager in the state, a highly recognized activist in woman's politics, and a dedicated social worker by profession. I was told that the chances of attracting the assistance of these very busy people was not likely, but their judgment and acceptance would encourage the approval of others in the party organization.

I knew that if I could be fortunate enough to get much-needed help from these folks, my chances of organizing an exciting campaign and realizing at least some small hope of election success would be enhanced greatly.

This couple agreed to talk to me, realizing that I was new to politics and no doubt feeling that it was important to know who might be seeking nomination in the coming primary election. I knew more about them than they knew about me and felt initially uncomfortable in the face of their experience and esteemed reputations. I knew that they both had managed successful campaigns for national as well as state and local offices and would size me up quickly as a viable candidate or a potential dud.

As we talked, I was somewhat uncomfortable; they questioned my motives and how I felt on various issues as well as what personal qualities and potential I felt I had for serving the people of Lane County, Oregon. They forced me to provide answers for questions I had not asked myself. I soon was relating ideas and strategies based on my past experience working with different groups of people. I felt that somehow, election in the democratic political manner lent itself best to candidates who were open, direct, and willing to share their ideas and prejudices with those who had to elect or reject them at the polls.

They must have seen me as a starry-eyed neophyte with little idea of the complexity of running a successful campaign, let alone the financial requirements and hours of hard work and often heartbreaking labor required to succeed. I realized that I was asking them to give assistance to a total stranger and was offering, seemingly, nothing in return.

As I later got to know them, I realized that at that first meeting, I presented some amount of the qualities that they saw of value in a candidate. They noticed a dedication to principles with which they agreed and the ability to be an effective representative of their own ideals for political changes both in issues and in strong democratic process.

I learned much in that initial meeting and was humbled by their agreement to help me and to assist in training others to form a strong campaign leadership committee. Their assistance proved invaluable in the months ahead, as an unusual campaign started and an assemblage of key campaign leaders met in my home.

Chapter 3
Campaign Strategy

The first meeting of the Owens campaign committee
was held in my home. This first session was really an
exploratory meeting out of which a formal campaign
organization would form. Because of the expectation
that many people new to politics would be attracted to
the campaign philosophy and strategy I wished to
employ, the idea was to use the more experienced
individuals (and therefore those already involved and
busy in other campaigns and issues), as advisors to
other very capable but less politically experienced
workers. The notion was that a lot of individuals new
to political campaigning would be willing to take on
responsibility if they had the back-up of more
experienced advisors. Thus, a campaign manager
was selected to team with an experienced advisor, as
well as a campaign treasurer, an issues chairman, a
fund-raising chairman, and other necessary leader to
perform the necessary tasks of running a successful
campaign. At this first meeting, I outlined my reasons
for seeking public office and the kind of campaign I
wished to lead and appealed to the support of
volunteers from a group of about thirty-five
participants. Most of the potential volunteers already
knew me, and a common philosophical perspective

on current issues seemed to be a major reason that people attended this first session.

As the meeting started, no one was committed to be involved in the campaign. They had been invited to hear a candidate, then determine if they wished to become involved, and, if so, in what way.

As I began to speak during this first campaign meeting of primarily close friends, I felt an excitement and a developing euphoria as I expressed my philosophical commitment to human issues in the coming campaign. I showed less interest in issues traditionally supported by big money industries and corporate interests generally. I felt that it was critically important that anyone working on the Owens campaign do so out of commitment to a similar philosophical perspective and that they see me as someone who would closely approximate their personal views and represent them in the way that they would themselves, if they were able. I wished to be viewed as a people's candidate, with openly expressed views on every possible issue. If anyone was to support me, I wanted them to do so because my perspective on issues closely resembled theirs and I could, in their judgment, be an effective legislator on their behalf.

Some of the issues about which I expressed concern and commitment to help resolve, included the following:

Environmental Issues. This topic included a stand against field burning, a particularly important issue to Lane County city residents who had difficulty tolerating the smoke generated by burning fields to "sanitize" them, following the harvest of grass seed.

Littler. Litter was a problem and I vowed to sponsor and do all that I could, to see a returnable bottle bill passed in Oregon. I was a member of the Oregon Environmental Council, an organization committed to an improved environmental for human beings and often at odds with industry and business overuse and abuse of resources.

Education. As an educator, I expressed strong support for educational financing, favoring 100 percent state level support for schools. I also expressed concern that public school education deserved support, and needed changing to become more student centered and less bureaucratic.

War in Vietnam. I had already demonstrated my activist views in opposition to the war in Vietnam and determined to do what was possible in the legislature to bring attention to the insensibility of continued fighting. This was a highly controversial issue, but most of the potential supporters in this first meeting were already behind this perspective.

Taxation. I favored a radical revision of taxation to make the income tax a more substantial part of total state funding, with a decreased emphasis on property tax. I also favored a more progressive tax schedule that benefitted low-income people.

As this first meeting continued, I felt a growing enthusiasm for my candidacy and an ever-increasing responsibility for becoming a truly representative politician with strong convictions, while maintaining a sensitivity to the views of others. At the same time, I began to feel somewhat uneasy with my own lack of knowledge about all the issues and about my own ability to justify the support that others seemed willing to give me. I began to feel an inkling of what it means to represent other people and to carry the load of others' expectations, knowing that no person can ever be as well informed and capable as an important situation might require. I was never to lose that feeling or the accompanying realization that for those people who supported me, and whom I represented, I was the best they had between them and the decisions affecting their lives in the legislative process. I was to find that it was important to be confident, always doing the best I could under the circumstances, with the awareness that a momentary inadequacy might hunt me later.

The result of the first "Owens for Legislature" meeting, was that the formal campaign structure was established and separate committees had met to "brainstorm" campaign strategies and relate their ideas to the total committee.

Some of the ideas suggested and later implemented included:

1. Try to locate an old school bus and refurbish it with volunteer labor, converting it into a "Voter Information Bus". This idea was to form an important central theme for the campaign.
2. Implement a "Call LeRoy" campaign, with a publicized telephone number with which citizens could make contract with the candidate, receive an issue-oriented campaign message, get instruction on how to be an effective citizen lobbyist, ask questions of the candidate, and join the Owens for Legislature effort, if interested.
3. Sponsor a series of fund-raising events, each focusing on widespread participation at low cost to participants. The idea was to raise necessary campaign funds through a broad base of small, individual donations. Supporters were encouraged to donate time and labor to the campaign, as well as dollars. The committee felt that it was cheaper to have things done by volunteer labor rather than purchasing it from others. These efforts were to include silk-screening of large posters by volunteer help, preparation of lawn signs and bumper stickers with volunteer help, and a wide variety of other campaign tasks including assistance in preparing issue statements, driving the bus, soliciting support door to door,

organizing campaign "events" to gain participation and support, and preparing mail-out materials.

Following this meeting, the separate committees went to work on the various ideas, and excitement for conducting an extensive volunteer campaign involving hundreds of people, grew. Separate committees were formed to find and refurbish a bus, paint signs, select campaign colors, organize campaign schedules, and appeal to the imagination and potential support of an increasingly broad base of voters' acceptance

Chapter 4
Throwing My Hat into the Ring

The campaign organization met following the official filing of candidates in the state capitol, an event that determined the opposition candidates and was to affect the style of campaigning through the primary and a very close general election in the fall. Oregon State has a nominating election, or primary, which enables each political party to select a single candidate for each position. The nominating, or primary, elections are held in May with the general election conducted six months later. Candidates announce their intention to run in the primary before the end of March, usually meaning that each campaign organization must continue to work for at least seven or eight months through the November election.

The final day for filing for the primary election in Oregon is characterized by a motley assemblage of candidates from all over the state at the capitol, most waiting to the last minute to file the Declaration of Intention to run. In most races, no one knows until the final deadline who is running for sure in each slot. In the election for State Representative, Lane County. Position #2, 1970, two candidates filed for the Democratic primary. For the same position on the

Republican ballot, the most notable contender was Bill Bowerman, a very popular and nationally known track coach at the University of Oregon. Mr. Bowerman was prominent in the U.S. Olympic team organization and was among the best-known people in the state. The Republican party had selected him to run, virtually assured that his name and familiarity would result in a secure seat on the Republican side of the aisle in the 1971-73 state legislature. Mr. Bowerman received much attention in the newspapers and on television upon his announcing his candidacy. His fame and easy accessibility to press coverage was to provide considerable consternation and frustration to my campaign.

But the announcement of Bill Bowerman's candidacy, rather than deflating the enthusiasm of my organization, encouraged a renewed dedication and actually helped gain support. Both Bowerman and I faced primary election opposition in their respective parties, but neither received serious opposition either during the campaign or at the polls. In fact, neither candidate was seriously expected to lose the primary, and certainly few people felt that anyone would stand a chance against Bill Bowerman in the general election in November – no one, that is, except a growing "Owens for Legislature Committee," which was about to launch a serious of inventive campaign strategies. The first of these was the formation of a broad-based and nonpartisan voter organization called the "Citizen Participation Committee."

Chapter 5
Getting Endorsed...

Campaigning in a large county such as Lane County, Oregon, requires extensive use of the media to gain sufficient name familiarity. With the voters in the Bowerman/Owens campaign, Bowerman already had name familiarity, making me a much less known underdog. To overcome this disadvantage, the our campaign knew that it must utilize the media effectively, even though campaign dollars were short, in order to make Owens "a household word."

Newspaper and television endorsements were recognized to be a valuable asset to any candidate. Because of the incidents mentioned previously, my campaign team did not expect an endorsement from the Eugene Register Guard but would have to try to get as much free publicity through press releases and, if possible (it seldom was), get pictures of the candidate on the most-read pages of the paper or on the six o'clock television news. Television was so expensive that the campaign committee had to rely on minimal coverage, primarily using free time provided by the stations for all candidates and purchasing some short announcements.

The Eugene Register Guard, the major newspaper of the county and the only Eugene City newspaper, as usual, made its endorsements of candidates a few days before the election. As expected, the track coach was endorsed, in spite of seemingly overwhelming (in the eyes of the Owens committee) evidence that he did not understand the issues and was running entirely on his track record. It was a surprise to me, then, when on the eve of the election, a large and expensive, nearly full-page ad, appeared in the Register Guard portraying a long list of campaign supporters (who had each contributed a special dollar or two to purchase the ad) and displaying my pictures, including the Voters Information Bus, and a strong statement of endorsement. At the same time, a number of letters were sent to the newspaper deriding the endorsement of Bill Bowerman and making a strong supportive statement for me.

Chapter 6
Volunteer Campaigning

Several volunteers contributed a large amount of personal time to assist with our campaign. One young man, recently discharged from military service, decided he wanted to work almost totally on the Owens committee. For months, he served as an unpaid campaign coordinator, living at our home, assuming such tasks as driving the Voter Information Bus, silk-screening posters, babysitting, and a wide range of other tasks that required practically day and night attention to campaign details. This volunteer later worked for several years in the state legislature and later with a state agency. His work with the campaign provided him an opportunity to learn a great deal about politics and also to use his considerable talents to assist in the election of someone whom he felt represented his perspective on most issues.

Another volunteer was a retired army colonel who had grown up in the state and wished to become involved in politics himself. By donating several days of his time, he gained access to legislative halls, provided a great deal of research help to a newly elected representative, and later ran successfully for public office.

Another individual volunteered to help with the campaign as a means to gain personal experience in politics, as well as to advance the causes of students such as herself. After the election, this young woman continued to donate at least one full day of her time each week and traveled to the legislature, receiving a firsthand, behind-the-scenes experience in the inner workings of the state legislature.

This individual was able to become acquainted with numerous legislators and, with a well-planned effort over a period of several years, was effective with other students in changing state law to require the governor to appoint a voting student representative on the State Board of Higher Education. Like many other students who participated in our campaign and later as volunteers in the legislature, they found the American political system to be open and responsive, while requiring dedication and perseverance of those who wish to change it.

Chapter 7
Citizen Participation Committee

The idea of a Citizen Participation Committee developed out of the desire to organize a broad base of support, cutting across traditional party lines. The idea had strong appeal as it would provide the means through which individual citizens could participate in an issue-oriented campaign and, in a representative way, participate in political decision making.

Many people do not relate to the partisan politics of political parties and are frustrated by a feeling of alienation toward the very structure that offers the means to correct their frustrations.

The Citizen Participation Committee allowed people of all ages and political persuasions an opportunity to participate in electing a candidate who, in most respects, represented their attitudes. Through this process, they could work constructively and affirmatively toward specific campaign objectives and, if successful in the election, have a spokesperson in their legislature as close as their private telephone.

The Citizen Participation Committee offered a wide range of opportunities for involvement, allowing each participant to work on those ideas and tasks that they felt most keenly about. As the committee organized, individuals from both political parties united in the common interest of electing a candidate to represent their ideas and attitudes in the state legislature. This notion did not minimize the candidate's strong political ties to the Democratic party but focused a broad base of support for electing a candidate for reasons that transcended partisan politics.

Involvement in the Citizen Participation Committee took several forms. Some members worked on voter registration, ensuring that the people who might wish to vote were properly registered in time to do so. Others concerned with voters' information could work on organizing the information to go into the Voter Information Bus.

Some individuals were interested in one or two issues and chose to develop position papers. An information file was set up to collect information on issues, making it available to the candidate and to other interested committee members. Another group worked on the idea of a citizen participation telephone system with recorded messages and references to voter information. Citizen participation meant citizen involvement in issues and procedures, which could make a difference in the decisions to be made in the legislature through better-informed voters and legislators.

Toward this end, the common thread was communication, and the "Call LeRoy" idea of using the telephone to communicate effectively with the voting constituency in a campaign and continuing the system after the election to enhance citizen legislative representation was an unusual idea.

Chapter 8
"Call LeRoy"

As a new candidate for public office, I found it difficult to see my name projected publicly on bumper stickers and signs and blasted on spot ads aver radio and television media. The "Call LeRoy" idea required the purchase of a telephone recording device that would allow the candidate to put a five-minute (or less) recorded message on tape each day and to invite all citizens to call the number for voter information.

The campaign committee located a sophisticated telephone record that would allow the recording of a message by using a special telephone line and number to "Call LeRoy." Interested citizens could dial the "Call LeRoy" number and receive instructions on how to vote, information on candidates and particularly where I stood on the issues, and information about election events.

The telephone recording device was constructed so that I could update the message by dialing a special recording number and record a timely message from anywhere reachable by telephone. Each day, then, I would place a brief message on the recorder home, always instructing the callers to dial me directly for conversation regarding issues and events related to the campaign.

As the candidate, I was somewhat uncomfortable about the prospect of having my family telephone ring at all hours of the day and night but was more concerned that I be an accessible candidate. For years, I had worked at public school positions where, on occasion, I had received prank calls from persons wishing to harass me or my family because of school-related problems.

On the other hand, I thought it important to prove my desire to be a responsive and accessible candidate and, hopefully, state representative. I assumed that people would respect my privacy by calling at a responsible hour. Mostly, I found this assumption to be true. The recording device, once activated, say, in the morning, provided the message automatically without anyone answering the telephone.

Since the "Call LeRoy" number was different from my home phone, interested individuals were instructed to call me personally. If their question was answered by message, they did not need to call.

An interesting thing happened. At all hours of the day and night, the half-ring of the recorded-message phone, indicating that someone was calling that special number, could be heard in my home. Only on rare occasions did the family phone ring following the message. If the ringing of the two phones coincided, I could be sure that someone was calling about the contents of the daily citizen participation message. Also, we found that people would ring the number for the recorded message at all hours of the night but would not bother me or my family by dialing my personal phone at that hour.

One exception I recall was a fellow calling long distance from a bar late at night. He had called the recorded message and had a bet with several of his cronies that no politician would tell you to call him personally and really mean it. From the background music and the slur of his words, I believed his explanation and knew that I helped to explode a myth about at least one politician: some candidates do care about what people think and recognize the importance of being accessible to those they represent.

Another means of communicating directly with my potential constituency was the Voter Information Bus.

CHAPTER 9
THE BUS

It seemed like a wild idea and a financially impossible one for the campaign committee to locate an old school bus that would run for the amount of money the campaign coffers could afford. I had insisted that with my meager income, any cost to the campaign would have to be raised by the efforts of our campaign committee. A couple of days after the campaign committee had met and suggested the bus idea, one of the committee members called to tell me that he had located an old bus that belonged to a hinterland church and they wanted $250 for it. He said the bus was a little rough, of 1948 vintage, but actually ran and still had all the seats in place.

Several of the committee members and myself decided to drive out and see this $250 find. It took us a bit of time to locate the bus, about twenty miles out of town, but we all enjoyed much joking and frivolity as we searched the back roads and contemplated what $250 would buy. When we finally found the bus, most of our jokes were realized. The bus was a 1948 flat-head Ford V-8 with more rust than fenders, but still had the rear-end blinking yellow warning lights intact, seats for 38 kids, and numerous panels of cracked glass, and was in much need of tender loving care. But it definitely presented a challenge. If any of us had realized what our imaginations had gotten us into, I doubt that we would have proceeded further. Our creative imagination, however, dominated our better judgment; the candidate loaned the committee $250, and the Voter Information Bus was born.

The metamorphosis of a thirty-eight-seat, almost ancient school bus into a mobile Voter Information Bus was interesting to behold. The committee had already decided that the campaign colors should be scientifically selected to express the best psychological encouragement for positives votes. This meant then that the predominant color of the bus was Euclid green, the standard color for the mammoth earth-moving equipment of the same name.

A committee member found that we could purchase gallons of this bright, almost yellow, green (some said pea green, others had different descriptions) from the local earth-moving machinery company. This particular shade of green was almost exactly the same color of new growth on Douglas fir trees, a nice comparison for an area abundant with this marvelous natural greenery. The committee thought that a campaign identifying with new growth and earth-moving equipment would certainly have a lot going for it. The accompanying color was to be a very dark green, which would be used for lettering and trim.

Selecting colors for the bus turned out to be minor by comparison to later considerations. Just the drive to town from its previous location of ownership demonstrated why the bus had been for sale for such a reasonable price. It did make the trip to town on its own but revealed an unusual thirst for gasoline, oil, and water. In fact, its thirst for these three ingredients was so demanding that it refused to run more than a few miles without renewed sustenance and encouragement.

The situation, however, appeared to be workable, as the campaign committee just happened to have a good mechanic volunteer. The bus could be mended and, with fortune, might limp its way through the campaign. The mechanic soon warned us, though, that mechanical death for the bus was inevitable as it had already outlived its expected longevity.

This news was less than heartening, but a sizable box was found into which large cans of oil, several gallons of water, and a conglomeration of tools and baling wire were deposited. This box of life-support items for the bus turned out to be an often called upon necessity for getting the "green monster" (as some called it) back home after a forage into the "outback" of Lane County.

Painting the bus was easy, thanks to four-inch brushes and agile volunteers. Little concern was voiced for preparation of the surface before copious floods of Euclid green were applied. The fact that portions of the bus were still damp from recent rain and the quick washing, along with all that body dirt from twenty-two years of faithful service, which insisted on remaining, resulted in little hesitation.

The result was a very light green, very noticeable, vehicle with a surface appearance of pebble corrugation and a recently painted look. The wheels, of course, were painted in the matching trim and huge letters suggesting that passing motorists "Call LeRoy," "Elect LeRoy Owens" and obtain free "Voter Information" were artfully applied to all sides. The result had to be the most unusual vehicle ever, and one that commanded attention everywhere it went. Spectators appeared amused as they read the signs.

The maiden voyage of the bus was to the Rhododendron Festival in Florence, a sixty-mile trip from the bus's home in Eugene, Oregon. The bus performed beautifully on the way to Florence, carrying me, my four children, my wife, and a picnic lunch. The entire trip from Eugene to Florence was downhill, of course, and the bus "rolled along" beautifully. I drove and tolerated the anxiety of the rest of the family, arriving in Florence too late for the brief festival parade but in time to drive the streets of town anyway, advertising our campaign.

The return trip exposed the temperament of the bus, often producing "vapor locks" and "boil overs." Frequent stops to cool off the engine (and passengers) and to add water to the thirsty radiator and oil to the crankcase, along with considerable vocal encouragement to the bus on the steep return grade, saw us home with no major difficulty.

The next "voyage" of the bus was to be the annual Lane County Fair parade and, after the 120-mile round trip to Florence, was anticipated to be a "piece of cake." Nobody thought to ask the bus, which by this time seemed to be developing a contemptuous attitude toward politics and a mechanical mind of its own.

The bus made many trips through community parades that campaign summer. None, however, matched the vehicle's behavior exhibited during the Lane County Fair parade. To amply demonstrate the candidate's interest in people, campaign workers' children were carefully preened and cleanly clothed to ride the bus and extend shiny and happy faces to the cheering crowd along the route. Because of the brevity of the parade route (leaving little chance of mechanical problems), the tow rope and other emergency mechanical paraphernalia were stored away behind the seats. The bus was carefully washed and later, with flags waving and banners flying, took its place in the lengthy parade line. The route was an easy one, but no one had counted on the vehicle's speed of one or two miles per hour for much of the five- or six- mile itinerary. No sooner had the bus pulled out of the parking lot with its happy load of passengers than an ominous blast of steam began to shoot from the dripping radiator, signaling a very hot engine. There was nothing to do but stay in line and pray for rain or some other act of God to end the parade before the bus exhibited its final gasp of steam. The driver found it impossible to delay or park such a lengthy bus along the parade route crowded on both sides with laughing expectant spectators who anticipated that the bus might gasp its last at any moment. They were anxious to see what would happen.

They didn't have to wait long. Just a half block from the judges' stand, on the most crowded avenue of the parade, the bus decided to take its final rest. By this time, the motor was so overheated, and so little water remained in the engine and radiator to cool it down, that the gas-line vapor locked, the engine stopped turning, and the campaign slowly coasted to a stop. There was nothing to do but to dig out the long tow rope, disembark all passengers except the driver, and pull and push the campaign bus past the judges' stand and several blocks beyond where a "turn off" could be found. By this time, all passengers, as well as the bus, were in a state of overheated exhaustion. Even the jugs of Kool-Aid could not adequately soothe the injured pride of the campaign workers and kids. Was there hope, some must have silently asked, for a campaign and a candidate that had to rely on people power rather than engine power to pull their candidate through the parade? There was some nervous laughing about the incident among the workers, but all were relieved when the bus, after an hour's rest and a cool drink of water, decided to carry its passengers back to their homes in proper style.

As I was to remark many times afterwards, "A funny thing happened on the way to the state legislature." Of all the events in the parade, the bus received more attention in the newspaper than most other entries. Dominantly displayed in a special parade pictorial was the bus, complete with a long tow rope and a visible display of "people power." In an election that certainly needed candidate visibility, the bus had come through. And in an election that pitted an unknown against a well-known track coach with an eight-to-one advantage in the polls, the bus became a visual reminder that in American politics, anything can happen and usually does. It also demonstrated that with a little bit of push and a little bit of pull, a tired bus can be encouraged to finish a parade, and even a campaign.

Chapter 10
Speaking to the Issues

One of the realizations I came to during that long campaign was that, too often, the specific issues upon which a candidate wishes to run are seemingly of little interest to the voters or to the newspapers they read. After having won the Democratic primary against a good opponent (who had little expectation of winning and was not negative about my outpolling him in the primary), I wanted to confront my general election opponent on the issues.

I was frustrated that "track coach" campaigning was working very well for my adversary and was doing nothing but assuring my anonymity as a candidate. All Bill Bowerman had to do was to express publicly his anger at not being able to park in his assigned parking place on the campus at the University of Oregon and he received a front-page story with a bold frame around it.

I received a small mention at the end of the article as the person against whom Coach Bowerman was running. The local (and only) newspaper periodically exhibited a fondness for Oregon's famous track coach and his candidacy for the state legislature.

CHAPTER 11
TRACK COACH POLITICS.

As the campaign progressed, Coach Bowerman continued to get easy press, but seldom related to any substantial issue. Press releases issued by the campaign would usually be printed, apparently in the guise of equity, but would be buried in the back pages of the paper.

Headlines for my opponent would often include his name, but my name usually appeared deep in the article with a reference to me as the opponent of Bill Bowerman. Then a strange phenomenon occurred. I began to receive phone calls, some from individuals who referred to themselves as "friends" of my opponent, who wished to see him remain a track coach and expressed concern that he would make a poor legislator. Some informal campaigning at teas and cocktail parties seemed to be centered around the theme: "Let's Keep Coach Bowerman as a Coach."

Supporters for Coach Bowerman had hired two young political science students to help manage his campaign. These bright young men, usually dressed in suits and exhibiting University of Oregon track colors of green and yellow, were often observed at campaign events. Apparently, the strategy of my opponent was to highlight his background as a University of Oregon coach, capitalizing on name familiarity by reminding people of his coaching reputation through use of the university colors and frequent references to coaching activities. This overt attention to name familiarity and little attention to the issues began to work to my advantage.

The campus chapter of the Sierra Club, apparently out of some concern that Coach Bowerman might be elected and resulting in environmental issues receiving little attention, organized a debate between the coach and myself. I was most pleased to accept the invitation.

The Sierra Club organized the Bowerman/Owens debate at noon, when numbers, as well as students, could easily attend. We had been asked prior to the meeting to speak briefly and then respond, in turn, to questions asked by a panel and the audience. We made personal statements expressing their philosophy, and a major difference between the two became evident.

Bill Bowerman expressed his desire to retire from coaching and to serve in the legislature as a way to complete his career. He expressed the feeling that the state had been good to him and that he now had a responsibility to serve in the legislature, thereby serving the people of the state.

My statement dealt with the recurring theme of our campaign, that citizens must have a greater say in the actions of government and that the citizens participation philosophy exhibited in the campaign, would carry through to the legislature. Also, I addressed a number of issues, knowing that the Sierra Club members would relate closely to my own environmentalist perspective.

During the question-and-answer portion of the debate, both candidates were asked their views on a number of issues, the first being their stand on the S.S.T. (supersonic transport). Bill Bowerman responded by admitting that he didn't know what the S.S.T. was and launched into a totally unrelated reply. I was delighted to be able to relate my own views on this issue, a prominent question before U.S. Congress and one that pitted environmentalists against industrial and military interests. The S.S.T. was clearly, in my judgment, an example of overt waste, misuse of resources, because of its highly inefficient construction and size.

The second issue that clearly separated the candidates on the issues, was field burning. Lane County farmers who grew grass seed and sanitized their fields by burning them following the harvest were at odds with townspeople who greatly outnumbered them. The smoke from field burning made breathing hazardous to health and generated great anger on the part of townspeople who had to breathe the noxious air. Bill Bowerman expressed support for farmers, saying that people had to have a right to make a living. This was not a satisfactory answer to the Sierra Club members present. In turn, I pointed out that this industry was of recent origin and that alternatives to burning fields had been proposed. I suggested that an immediate ban to field burning be mandated by the legislature and that if a tax on the production of grass seed could be used for research to find alternatives to field burning, I would favor such legislation. Needless to say, the campaign was enhanced by this debate, as evidenced by letters to the editor and an increase in campaign contributions from Sierra Club members.

Another incident in the "track coach" campaign that caused me considerable anxiety was an article in the national magazine Sports Illustrated, which featured a story about Steve Prefontaine, a fantastic long-distance runner who had been "discovered" by Bill Bowerman. Steve had enrolled in the university and was making an international reputation for himself as a promising record setter in the sub-four-minute mile (and who later met an untimely death in an automobile accident). To prepare for this article, the author had interviewed Bill Bowerman at length and subsequently reported an incident that was to become a small problem for our campaign.

Bill Bowerman related to the author of the article an incident in which a rock-truck driver had, on several occasions, knocked over his mailbox near his home in rural Lane County. He stopped the driver and asked him not to knock over a mailbox again. Subsequently, when he found his mailbox on the ground once more, Bill Bowerman took the matter into his own hands.

He reportedly attached one or two sticks of dynamite to the mailbox and, as a result, blew the wheel off the rock truck. The article did not mention whether the mailbox had been placed in the proper location for mail pick-up and delivery or what the interchange between the truck driver and Bill Bowerman's action was. The truck driver was not hurt, apparently. The incident provided the author of the Sports Illustrated article with a means of relating the individuality and self-direction of Coach Bowerman. Of course, the article was widely read nationally, as well as in Lane County, Oregon, and, of course, by workers of both of our campaigns.

When a university student presented the article to me with great glee, I knew I had to make some statement to my campaign organization, or the Bowerman bombing incident could be as much trouble to me as it was to him. I knew that any such accusation and attack on a much-revered public figure such as Bill Bowerman would not be met positively by many people. Therefore, I called a meeting of the campaign organization and vehemently directed that no one was to use the incident in any way to discredit Bill Bowerman or to use it to gain favor for the campaign.

Only one related situation developed during the campaign, but it indicated how volatile that particular incident could have been. A high school student, gathering information to debate another student as an Owens versus Bowerman presentation for a speech class, called me to collect information and to ask me about the dynamite incident. He had read the article of note in the Sports Illustrated magazine and wanted to know what truth there was to it. I could only refer him to the article and to Bill Bowerman, explaining that I knew nothing other than what I had read in the article.

Several days later, I received a very irate call from the student's teacher, accusing me of possibly inventing the story. I referred him to the article and suggested he call Bill Bowerman if he needed information, and I told him that I had no intention of using the article in the campaign and had instructed others working with me to disregard the article entirely. The teacher thanked me for my attitude. Having worked with the school district some years before, I was aware that this teacher came from the town's most ardent track high school and that Bill Bowerman had many friends and admirers among the staff and student body. In no manner did I wish to besmudge his track record. It spoke for itself.

Besides the school speech incident, someone entirely unknown to me did write a letter to the editor of the local newspaper mentioning the mailbox bombing incident and urging support for LeRoy Owens. I am sure that my decision to disregard that unfortunate incident was wise and would have gained me no personal or political advantage.

Further, such action on my part would have been completely out of character with what was later characterized by some as the best legislative campaign in the history of the county. This incident demonstrated to me that the candidate is finally responsible for anything and everything that occurs in the name of his or her campaign. I had excellent campaign advisors and managers, who all totally agreed with my position in this matter.

As the campaign progressed, I came to know my opponent better and genuinely liked him. Also, I came to realize that he was a product of an exciting career that had left him poorly informed about many of the issues that legislators would be expected to decide upon. I came to see him as a good person who was somewhat tired of a successful career and ready to make a change.

The Republican friends who encouraged him to run did him a disservice. In their fervor to retain a Republican seat they had sought a candidate who would be electable and one who might have been expected to "play the game" and defer to party leadership for guidance in determining important issues. This minor election choice provided the voters an opportunity to choose between a relatively young, issue-oriented candidate with clear-cut stands on issues and a mature, well-known public figure who had little grasp of the issues, but was, nonetheless, a nice guy. It was my endeavor, as the campaign continued, to focus heavily on issues and expose my opponent's ignorance of voters' concerns. In an attempt to do this, the Owens committee called for a public meeting, at which time I would "speak to the issues."

Chapter 12
Town Meeting Politics

My motivation to run rested strongly on a personal desire to become an effective agent for change through the most potentially effective means I knew of: serving in the state legislature. As the campaign progressed, I became increasingly frustrated that voter interest seemed to focus more on the irrelevant issues of "track coach" campaigning than on the substantive issues of critical importance to Lane County citizen. I saw my responsibility as a candidate, to project my ideas and stand on all issues, whether anyone wanted to listen or not.

The city of Eugene has a public meeting building at which meetings can be arranged and attended by large groups of people. The campaign arranged for this meeting hall, advertised in the local paper, and announced that I would present my views on every issue I could think of and openly and honestly try to answer any questions asked from the audience. Of course, the press was invited in the hope that this great issue meeting would be reported in the media, thereby focusing campaign rhetoric on the real issues.

About fifty people, nearly all campaign workers, attended the meeting and listened to their candidate talk for an hour and a half about local, state, and national issues, many of which were of little direct concern to the audience. Not a single member of the press attended. While I gained much intellectual therapy from the engagement, few listeners were surprised by my stands on the issues. They already knew. What the campaign committee had hoped to happen had not. A ground swell of interest in the issues was not generated by the meeting.

I left the meeting with some feeling of satisfaction for having at last been able to expose my prejudices to all who would listen. I did feel considerable disappointment (which I had expressed in the meeting) that the press was not in attendance and that apparently the local media, and perhaps too many voters, were not really interested in where the candidate stood.

The following morning, at work, I received a call from the political editorial writer, a reported friend of Coach Bowerman, for the local newspaper. He was extremely upset with me and wondered "just what I thought I was doing" in having a large number of people call him directly and demand an accounting for why the newspaper had not covered the meeting the night before. He had received, he said, about ten calls and was "sick and tired of it." He added, in good historical rhetoric, "If you can't stand the heat, why don't you get out of the kitchen?" It took some time for him to run down adequately enough to explain to me what had been happening. Apparently, several of my campaign supporters were incensed that their candidate received such short shrift by the local media, especially the newspaper, and took it into their hands to correct the situation. One ardent supporter the campaign treasurer, and a lifelong Republican) was an example of several phone calls. She had "read out" the editor in colorful and explosive language, leaving him somewhat bewildered and increasingly angered.

When I was able to piece together what had happened, I did as the editor asked and "called off my dogs." Rather than being angered by the editor's call, I was amused.

Later, the telephone action was described by my campaign treasurer who realized that I would not have approved of the action. But she and others had decided it was time to do something anyway. No one really expected the heavily Republican-oriented newspaper to endorse an upstart Democrat against the local hero and Republican track coach. "But," she said, "the least they could do is cover your public meetings, just as they do the Republicans'." I had a lot of respect for the power of the local editor and wasn't altogether pleased about his attitude toward me, but I was more pleased with the attitude of my campaign workers. Though I didn't agree with their tactics, I completely agreed with their intentions.

The campaign trail, in Oregon, is a long one between the primary (in May) and the general election (in November). As the months went by, I learned a terrific amount about representative politics and the latent desire of most citizens to be well represented politically. I came to understand that most voters do not look at party politics as the beginning step to deciding how to vote on candidates. I found that people were not disinterested in the issues but were foremost interested in the kind of people campaigning, their attitudes, and the kind of human model they presented.

I found many people willing to support me, even though I spoke openly in opposition to their perspective on a particular issue. Why? Because they somehow knew that the issues of the day were not all the legislative process was about. The voters I met mostly wanted to understand the kind of person they were deciding to vote for or against and seemed to primarily want someone they could relate to. I began to understand the notion that our elected bodies finally are a reflection of the attitudes and aspirations of the constituencies they represent.

Other incidents occurred throughout the campaign that brought a lump to my throat and reinforced my dedication to be the best candidate and, hopefully, the best representative in the interests of the people I was asking to elect me.

One good friend on the campaign committee decided that he could help the effort by combining the best sixteen-millimeter film footage he had collected over the years in Lane County. With his son providing the accompaniment by guitar, this friend spliced together a beautiful film on Lane County scenes, had me narrate it, added footage of me and my family in our home city of Eugene, and produced a beautiful environmental and campaign film.

Another campaign worker (a Republican), was a good carpenter and offered to provide the materials and build the shelving and containers required to convert the bus into a voter information center.

Printing campaign signs would have been extremely expensive, but a campaign worker donated his time to do this technical task that would have cost a meager campaign valuable dollars.

A talented nine-year-old singer and friend of my youngest son offered to make a radio jingle and record it. This contribution produced one of the most catchy and valuable campaign jingles imaginable.

It would have been too expensive, probably prohibitive, to purchase large campaign posters and to have signs made to attach to the top of vehicles for street advertising. One supporter volunteered to convert a candidate picture, through a silk-screening process, to an enlarged poster. These same posters were used to advertise events, for lawn signs, and for car signs throughout the campaign.

It is impossible to enumerate all of the ideas that go into a campaign effort involving several hundred people. Efforts to get out mass mailings require hundreds and thousands of hours of time addressing and stamping envelopes and sorting mail for efficient distribution. Many campaign supporters are required to host coffees and luncheons, to set up meetings, and to make telephone contacts for the many tasks necessary to run an effective campaign.

It bothered me that so many people were doing so much to elect a single candidate. How can any elected official live up to the expectations of those who helped elect him, let alone to meet the expectations of a total constituency of over thirty thousand people? I began to understand that people were working not just to elect me, but in an attempt to ensure that better government would result from their efforts.

The candidate, in this regard, serves as the identity, or focal point, of the dreams and aspirations of a lot of different people. Campaign workers, by and large, work out of enlightened self-interest. They work on a particular candidate's campaign because they identify with what that individual represents, perhaps on single issues, or to encourage their own perspectives to be directly represented in legislative halls.

I found myself wrestling with the philosophical question of "Does a candidate represent his own conscience, or does he represent the will of his constituency?" I answered this question by determining to know as much as possible about the issues and developing positions that I could relate to voters and in so doing, enable them to choose candidates according to their stance on ideas important to them.

The difficulty was, of course, in knowing enough about each issue to be absolutely sure my position was correct. I vowed to do the best I could to understand each issue, to speak forthrightly, even in the face of controversy, and to ask the voters to share a responsibility for my actions by helping to inform me on any issue important to them. This approach, I was to find, did not always result in my assuredly making the correct choice on every issue. It did help me sleep at night.

A candidate or a representative of the people must assume a position of responsibility in making decisions that are considerably beyond the scope of most individual citizens alone. The concern over these questions helped me to formulate an idea to give each voter a more direct, issue-oriented representation. But that is another story to be told a bit later.

Chapter 13
Election Night Fever

The election night tradition in Lane County called for a series of political parties and a final assemblage of candidates and their workers at the Eugene Hotel to count the final returns (vicariously), imbibe in postelection libations, and play election quarterback, after the fact.

On election night, November 3, 1970, a large crowd of volunteers assembled to "sit with" the candidate and count votes reported by television. As the first returns came in, Coach Bowerman maintained a healthy lead, and there appeared to be little hope that the election would go otherwise. But as the night wore on and votes from outlying precincts, as well as late returns from the city's areas, were reported, the differences, in votes tallied between Bowerman and I steadily decreased.

Although the tally became closer, the possibility of a swing in my favor seemed unlikely. I found myself reassuring campaign workers with long faces, and though I felt an impending disappointment I reiterated my earlier statements concerning my motivation for running. Before announcing my intention to run, I had questioned my motivation and determined that I would run to win, but that the process of campaigning itself would provide sufficient justification for the effort to be personally productive. I felt that what I had to say about the issues and, should I lose, the opportunity to speak my mind and to be able to learn and develop personal effectiveness for the future was sufficient reason to be a candidate.

Though I reiterated those words as an apparently losing candidate on election night, I nonetheless felt the sting and agony of potential defeat. It was fine for me to express the importance of having participated in a highly visible, issue-oriented campaign and say the process was worth it. It was like saying "It isn't whether you win or lose, but how you play the game."

The direction of the hard work of the campaign committee and myself for the past eight months, had been to win the election and to secure a seat in the state House of Representatives for an individual representative of the political aspirations of a large group of people. I found myself uneasy to be preparing myself for two very opposite responses at the same time. I wanted to win the election but at the same time wished to prepare myself for a dignified defeat. As it turned out, I needn't have worried.

At about ten-thirty, after the polls had been closed for about two hours, the returns showed that I had caught up, and through the rest of the evening, I maintained a slight edge over my opponent. Every campaign worker must have felt that he or she had personally won the election. With my election, Democrats in Lane County had swept all six legislative seats that year. And Coach Bowerman was able to retain his coaching duties. I wonder if he didn't feel, in his legislative defeat, that he had won after all.

CHAPTER 14
SERVING AS A LEGISLATOR

Every newly elected legislator must feel some of what I felt after winning my first election. Never before had I felt such a burden of responsibility and personal autonomy at the same time. Suddenly, my personal mail increased about one hundredfold. Much of my mail came addressed to the "Honorable" Representative LeRoy Owens.

I began to understand the importance of lobbying, both from a perspective of individuals and groups who wished to effect changes through the political system and to the legislator who needed good information upon which to make decisions.

The house rules of the Oregon legislature require that all representatives vote "yes" or "no" on all issues, and that "taking a walk" and avoiding having to make an uncomfortable or potentially politically unwise decisions is nearly impossible. The continuing responsibility of the legislator is to know enough about each issue to vote conscientiously and in the best interest of his or her constituency at all times. Without good information, wise decisions are difficult to determine.

In the short period of time between the November elections and the beginnings of the legislative sessions in January, much activity took place. Both parties had to caucus and determine the best strategy for organizing the legislature for the benefit of their party.

Not all issues are political, from a political party perspective, but holding dominant power provides the fortunate party with enough votes to ensure passage of legislation proposed by the party platform. The payoff to working for the election of party members is to gain sufficient control to be able to appoint committee chairmen and guide the process of critical legislation through the House and senate to eventual passage.

Also, individual legislators and coalitions of legislators work for passage of their own pet legislation, either to satisfy themselves and their reasons for seeking election, or the interests of their constituency, or both Like others, I had a number of bills that I wished to have prepared and submitted through the legislature as early as possible.

Preparing legislation in the Oregon state legislature is assisted by a group called the Legislative Council. As a duly elected legislator, I was able to call the Legislative Council office and ask them to prepare legislation, hoping to have several important bills ready for introduction at the beginning of the legislative session. I decided that it was important to move fast and initiate legislation that addressed key issues upon which I had campaigned. I was later to discover that other newly elected legislators did likewise, and, in some cases, an overabundance of similar legislation was prepared and awaiting introduction. The Legislative Council was able to copy (in some cases only making slight changes) bills introduced by one legislator for others as well.

Also, the historical files in the Legislative Council contained hundreds of bills that had been introduced and had gone nowhere in the past. A number of these were brushed off each session to meet the requests of legislators. In my case, however, several original ideas had to be drafted into legislation that seemed to be entirely new and to this date have not been heard of since. But more of that later…

Besides all of the reorganization of the legislature along party line, there were a number of personal decisions to be made. My wife and I had agreed that we would rent a home in Salem, sixty miles north of our home in Eugene, for the duration of the legislative session.

We found a number of houses available, as Salem residents often wish to get out of town during the volatile legislative sessions. We were able to find a couple to look after our home and to look after our oldest son who chose to remain in Eugene for school. He had opted to join us on weekends. Activities initiated during the campaign, such as the Citizen Participation Committee and the "Call LeRoy" phone message system were continued and provided a communication link between my campaign and election was enhanced with a challenge to the election results by candidate Bowerman and the Republican party.

The election had been close, with only about two hundred and fifty votes separating the candidates, so that a challenge was probably a good idea. Both parties sent observers to challenge ballots as they were recounted in the County Clerk's office, but no major or even minor discrepancies were uncovered.

In the period between the election and the session, political attention in the press focused considerably on the question of how the legislature might and could be organized. The Republicans had maintained a comfortable margin of seats in the House of Representatives. In the senate, although the Democrats held a few seats' advantage, a coalition of Republicans and rural Democrats resulted in selection of coalition leadership of that body.

This meant that it would be exceedingly difficult for Democrats to get key legislation passed and particularly meant that I would serve as a minority party freshman legislator. I was soon to learn that getting elected did not mean that my vote would count the same weight as other elected representatives. In rule by majority vote, the dominant rule of legislative process, obtaining more than half the votes on any issue is required for passage. Minority party members usually found themselves on the short side of the vote on major controversial issues. Also, being a member of the minority party meant few Democrats held positions of influence as chairmen of committees or the all-important roles of leadership held only by majority party members.

I quickly realized that much of my own effectiveness would have to come through the power of personal persuasion behind the scenes, and probably not through heavy politic plays with too few votes to win the final battles. I was to find out that not all Republicans or Democrats necessarily lined up true to the dictates of their own party leadership. In these instances, coalitions could form around issues, and, in some cases, the party leadership specifically kept away from party stands in such controversies.

Another aspect of personal effectiveness that I was to come to appreciate was representing constituents as a legislative advocate communicating directly with the state bureaucracy. I found my position as an elected official particularly helpful in assisting constituents who had difficulties with various state agencies. All state agencies were dependent on legislated support for their budgets and were usually more than willing to work closely with elected officials of either party.

Now, as the opening of the 1971 Oregon state legislature approached, I found myself even busier, if possible, than I had been during the campaign. I approached the opening day of the session with great anticipation and some anxiety.

CHAPTER 15. LEARNING THE LEGISLATIVE PROCESS

The fifty-sixth legislative assembly opened with much fanfare and pageantry and with a considerable number of new faces in attendance. I was personally proud and a little bit scared as I observed and participated in the proceedings.

As time went on, I was to learn that my colleagues and I represented quite closely, the composite opinions and attitudes of our state. I found that we all tended to agree more often than disagree, and most of the legislation we were to consider would not really be controversial in nature but would be housekeeping issues necessary to the continuing operation of the state.

As the days and weeks went on, I found myself becoming very tired physically but with little loss of motivation and dedication. It helped to have my wife working directly with me as a secretary, both providing the necessary financial support for our family and as an unquestioned source of loyalty and support when needed.

Our lifestyle became one of early rising in the morning, my catching the bus in front of our West Salem house then arriving at my office early to read newspapers and constituent mail.

Meanwhile, Mary Jo would prepare breakfast for our school-age children, deliver them by station wagon to school, and arrive at 8:00 a.m. for a heavy schedule of secretarial and administrative chores.

Mornings were taken up with early committee meetings, caucus sessions, and usually a morning legislative session beginning at ten or eleven o'clock.

Afternoons were taken up with committee meetings and legislative sessions, usually until five or six o'clock in the evening. Mary Jo would take the bus home from the capitol in the evening in time to meet our children, prepare dinner, and maintain a semblance of ordinary family life.

I would return home following late afternoon meetings, usually to return to an evening committee meeting, caucus session, or political event, probably sponsored by a lobbying group. We soon found ourselves somewhat adjusted to the rigorous time schedules required.

I began to focus increasingly on the legislative process itself, the key to effectiveness in the legislature. I found that keeping up with the flow of legislation to be considered each day was a monumental task. Just reading the bills themselves was nearly impossible. Of necessity, I relied on others for information and too often was not completely satisfied with my own "yes" or "no" vote.

I found myself signing on as a sponsor with others to get bills introduced, realizing sometimes that this legislation would never get out of its initial committee, but that it was important to its sponsor to be introduced. At the same time, I was introducing my own pet legislation and asking others to sign on as well. Each day, a number of newly introduced bills would be "thrown into the hopper" and distributed to various committees for consideration.

It did not take me long to realize that this distribution process was the beginning and the end of most pieces of legislation. The Speaker of the House could direct the bill to a close political associate and committee chairperson who, in turn, would "kill it" or "pass it out" through a friendly committee structure almost completely controlled by the party leadership and its head, the Speaker himself.

To a minority party freshman legislator, my pet bills found themselves at the mercy of the Speaker, who exhibited a most undemocratic disdain for freshman legislators of the opposite party. Nonetheless, I felt it necessary on several occasions to approach the Speaker and ask for assistance in getting bills I had personally introduced into committees where I hoped they would get fair hearings.

In all instances, I found the Speaker courteous and friendly, but I found his actions in nearly all such matters demonstrative of his general uncooperativeness for freshman legislators of the other party. It was little consolation that my own anger and disrespect were shared by practically all members of my own party and a considerable number of the Speaker's own political party associates.

Some of the important legislation that I introduced or helped to sponsor is described in the following pages.

CHAPTER 16
THE CAMP ADAIR "GIVEAWAY"

Even before the fifty-sixth legislature got underway, I was to become embroiled in one of the hottest issues to face the session. A statewide organization, called the Council of the Poor, asked me to attend a conference of their organization just prior to the meeting of the legislature. This group had been trying, without success, to obtain use of a surplus air force base called Camp Adair, near Corvallis, Oregon.

Camp Adair had twice been purchased by the U.S. government for an air base and for the second time was declared surplus property, thus becoming available for other governmental use. Already, the governor and several other leading politicians had written letters declaring that the Camp Adair property was of no value to the state at that time, and each endorsed the proposal of a private college in California, U.S. International University (U.S.I.U.), who sought donation of the property for their educational use.

The law affecting U.S. government surplus property required that a hierarchy of uses for such property be considered. In this instance, if the Camp Adair property was not deemed usable for the state, it then was to become available for transfer to private educational groups.

The Council of the Poor found out about the potential availability of the property and wished to be able to make use of some of the buildings and perhaps the nearly new Capehart family housing units. The council of the Poor had not gained the support of the governor's office or the support of the U.S. senators and representatives of the state, as each had already been approached by U.S. International University and were supporting its application.

At the pre-legislative meeting of the Council of the Poor, I was confronted with the statement, "You politicians are all the same. You promise to help poor people, but you don't do anything." I honestly didn't know what to do but promised to do what I could to find out what had happened to the application of the council for the Camp Adair property. The Council of the Poor provided me with a voluminous file of information, including copies of letters from several of the Oregon U.S. congressional delegation supporting the U.S.I.U. proposal. How the group was able to obtain these letters, I don't know, but they were certainly incriminating, and potentially embarrassing to each elected official.

The problem I faced was what to do with the information and to decide what possible action might be taken by the legislature to ensure that the property was not "given away" without due consideration of the potential use to the citizens of Oregon. I didn't know it at the time, but I was about to stir up a hornet's nest and to quickly discover the power of the press to react when the potential interest of the public is disregarded.

I was able to sort out the ingredients of this issue, but as a green, freshman legislator, I needed help. I wisely sought out the counsel of my political colleagues, particularly Representative Harl Haus, the newly elected minority leader. After some consideration, Representative Haus suggested that I introduce a memorial, a measure that is used to ask the U.S. Congress to do something but carries little more than persuasive weight.

Representative Haus saw the potential political dynamite that this issue might ignite considering that the governor, Tom McCall, a prime potential candidate for the coming U.S. Senate race (and a Republican), might be much embarrassed by having supported the outside interests of U.S. International University against the possible interests of citizens of the state for use of the Camp Adair Property. I asked Legislative Council to help prepare the memorial and made an appointment to see the governor.

I had always liked Governor McCall, though I had never had an opportunity to meet him directly. I found him most gracious and personable, and appreciative that I had come to him before introducing the Camp

Adair Memorial. He agreed that the issue could be somewhat embarrassing. I told him that I assumed his advisors had prepared the recommendation that he had made by letter, supporting the U.S.I.U. proposal and stating that he saw no immediate use for the property by the state of Oregon.

I explained to the governor that I had no interest in causing him political embarrassment and that I would keep him apprised of any information that might be helpful in resolving the issue. I suggested that his office had made a mistake, and that if the issue could be corrected in some manner other than politically, I was certainly in favor of such action. I left the governor's office convinced that he had not really been aware of the incriminating nature of the letter he had signed (or someone had signed for him) and that he would do what he could to resolve the issue short of legislative action. After leaving the governor's office, I called my first press conference as an installed legislator and prepared a release for that occasion.

Ordinarily, the capitol press corps does not respond with great enthusiasm to press conferences called by newly elected, minority party, freshman legislators. In this instance, however, the Camp Adair issue had become a cause celebre of the Salem Statesman newspaper but so far, public indignation concerning the issue was hardly aroused.

After making opening remarks and passing out the press release announcing the introduction of the Camp Adair Memorial, I was asked several key questions. "How was a memorial, the least powerful of legislative actions, going to accomplish anything? Wasn't the issue already out of the hands of the state?"

Other questions indicated a great deal of interest in this issue, and I clearly realized I had a tiger by the tail. I explained that the application for U.S. International University was already being processed, and the deadline for competitive applications had passed. I reiterated my own disdain for the property being "given away" to a private, out-of-state group, when so many potential uses to the citizens of the state existed.

The reaction of the news media to this press conference and to subsequent statements made by me regarding the Camp Adair issue, taught me much about the operation and usability of a public press media. Certainly, this issue was one of considerable interest to most citizens, and it smacked of possible collusion and wrongdoing on the part of elected politicians. At no time did I feel that there had been any intentional wrongdoing on the part of any of Oregon's elected officials, but rather oversight and lack of sensitivity to the public interest had been demonstrated.

Following the introduction of the Camp Adair Memorial, the Speaker of the House assigned the measure to the State and Federal Affairs Committee, a "hip-pocket" committee of the Speaker, which was shared by his caucus assistant, the Republican whip. This assignment provided maximum control of the process for consideration of the Camp Adair Memorial by the Speaker himself.

As the weeks went by, it became evident that neither the Speaker nor the chairman of the State and Federal Affairs Committee, had any intention of scheduling a hearing that might be of potential embarrassment to their political party and to Governor McCall, their Republican figurehead and leader. Also, Governor McCall was considering running against Senator Mark Hatfield, and the House leader had to be cautious about intraparty rivalry, which might result from uncovering the action of the governor and other Republicans in this matter.

Following the announcement of the introduction of the Camp Adair Memorial, a reporter from the Salem Statesman asked to see me and related that his newspaper was very interested in this issue and had some time ago assigned him to do an investigative report. This reporter had collected a great deal of information and had also been in continual contact with the Council of the Poor. He shared with me his perspective that my contentions regarding the issue were correct, and that the U.S. International

University proposal had been processed with far too little attention to the interests of the citizens of the state of Oregon, and that there might be a whole lot more to the issue than appeared on the surface. He agreed to work closely with me in sharing information that either of us could interchange without limiting the integrity of either of us performing our respective jobs.

I found him to be most helpful and completely trustworthy. I found this type of positive working relationship with a member of the press to be generally the case and possible with most members of the press corps. His interest was to find and report the truth, as was mine. I knew I could not pass legislation to correct this matter, but I might be able to bring enough attention to the issue to get it adequately resolved at other governmental levels.

Following the press release, I began to get a flood of mail from individuals who knew something about U.S. International University or about the Camp Adair issue itself. I began to see the U.S.I.U. organization more in light of a real estate holding company, than a private educational university.

I found that they held titles to about fourteen other former military installations. Also, I discovered that they had made a proposal to accept title to a private college in Hawaii and several hundred acres of pineapple farmland belonging to that institution. As time went by, I became increasingly frustrated in not being able to get straight answers either from the U.S.

Department of Health, Education and Welfare (H.E.W.) or out of my own Oregon House of Representatives leadership. It appeared that the chairman of the State and Federal Affairs Committee intended to "bury" the memorial, and after two months, still had not scheduled a hearing of the proposal.

At that point, I went to the chairman of the committee and insisted that a hearing be scheduled. This he did, scheduling it about as far ahead as he could. I understood his concern better when I received a call from a young lawyer from Senator Hatfield's office in Washington, D.C. He explained that the senator was very interested in the issue.

The senator's assistant asked to meet with me and to receive any information I could give to him regarding the issue, particularly any information on Governor McCall's activities relating to Camp Adair. I agreed to meet with him but was most cautious about generating political ammunition that might be used against Governor McCall in a subsequent senatorial race. The plot thickened.

Finally, public and political pressure built up sufficiently that a hearing had to be scheduled. When I received no satisfaction in getting a hearing on the docket, I called a press conference and made this information and some other tidbits available to the press corps. In repeated calls to the office of the secretary of H.E.W., I tried to determine the status of the U.S.I.U. application. At one point, I was told by the spokesman for the secretary of H.E.W. that the application was still under consideration. This was on a Friday, and on the following Monday, I was able to ascertain that a title to the property had already been processed in the courthouse in Albany, Oregon, deeding the property to the U.S. International University over a twenty-year period. Once again, I called a press conference.

After months of struggling to find the truth on this issue, I was infuriated that I, a member of the Oregon State House of Representatives, would be lied to by federal bureaucrats, and that while the Oregon legislature was still considering the Camp Adair issue, the federal government was in fact, at the same time, deeding the property to U.S.I.U.

I announced at the press conference that a mistake might have been made but that I believed that I had been lied to. Subsequently, members of the press checked my information and found that, indeed, U.S.I.U. had been granted deed to the property. This meant that over a hundred acres of prime Willamette Valley farmland, air base facilities, family housing, and other potentially usable structures had been given to a private, nonprofit corporation outside of the state of Oregon to the disregard of numerous applications made by Oregon citizens.

I was mad as hell, and so were newspapers all over the state. I must admit that though I was extremely indignant, I knew I had a political "bull by the tail" and I was enjoying my role as a burr under the saddle of those who had allowed the Camp Adair "giveaway" to occur.

During the process of transfer of title of the property (unknown to anyone in the legislature, as near as I know), hearings were finally held by the State and Federal Affairs Committee, and hundreds of interested citizens attended.

A vice-president of U.S. International University came up from California and made a rather impressive appearance at the hearing. He explained that U.S.I.U. intended to open a campus and had already offered jobs to a number of Oregon residents who wished to teach with the institution.

I had already received mail from some of these individuals, a few that I knew professionally, and was disheartened that with all the trouble our private state institutions were having to keep up enrollments and maintain financial solvency, yet another institution was originating under our noses and acquiring the physical resources of Camp Adair. Oregon State University, located on the edge of Camp Adair, was one of the applicants for use of the property.

Their application had not been seriously considered while that of U.S. International University had been encouraged by the governor and other officials. I could not know, even though the issue appeared to be lost, that other activity was happening behind the scenes in the governor's office.

It is a tradition during Oregon legislative sessions that the governor and his wife host a series of dinners for the members of the House of Representatives and Senate. The governor's "mansion" in Oregon is a very ordinary home of insufficient size to host more than a few individuals at a time. I had not been in the governor's home before the invitation to attend one of his series of legislative dinners and was surprised to be ushered into a remodeled basement with low ceilings, and hardly suitable for the entertaining expected to be carried on by the governor and his family. I was also impressed by the lack of ostentatiousness.

During the basement cocktail hour, the governor indicated that he would like to see me and drew me into the laundry room, cautioning me to watch my head on the clotheslines. Governor McCall was even taller than my six-foot-four-inch frame, and we both had to bend toward each other to carry on a conversation. I was delighted with what he had to say.

"You will be happy to hear, LeRoy, that you have won the Camp Adair issue," the governor stated. "Today I asked the president of U.S.I.U. to return the title to the Camp Adair property to the federal government, and he has agreed to do so. Also, I am going to call a press conference announcing this information and that I am asking Senator Hatfield to take over responsibility for deciding what should be done with Camp Adair."

This last remark of Governor McCall's indicated the irritation he must have felt with having a fellow Republican party member, Senator Mark Hatfield, waiting eagerly to use the Camp Adair issue against him, should he oppose him in the coming senatorial election. I was proud of what the governor had done, and that in spite of his earlier recommendation for disposal of the Camp Adair property, he had the gumption to change his mind and to take action to resolve the issue in the interest of the people of the state.

I was even more proud of my involvement in the issue, and I didn't even mind that the Camp Adair Memorial was tabled in the State and Federal Affairs Committee, and thereby failed to pass out of the legislature. What was important to me was that the interests of the people of the state were recognized by the resolution of this issue behind the scenes. Senator Mark Hatfield did make "political hay" of the issue by holding a series of hearings prior to his next election, resulting finally in Camp Adair's being utilized by several state agencies and groups, including the state police, a Brown Study Center (for Chicano people), and a game preserve. I attended one of Senator Hatfield's "hearings" and was carefully scheduled to speak after five o'clock, after the television cameras and other news people had left to meet evening deadlines.

This issue did not make me popular in Republican party circles, but it did help me to become better acquainted with the legislative process and to begin to make good political friends with thoughtful members of both political parties.

Chapter 17
A State "Jobs" Program

While serving on the Welfare Subcommittee of the House Health, Education and Welfare Committee, I became increasingly concerned with the indignity of our state and federal welfare program. Even after an objective evaluation was made of the employability of persons on public welfare and the proof that almost no fraud was found in administration of this program, feelings still persisted that public welfare provided an easy handout to undeserving freeloaders. This feeling resulted in applicant screening and monitoring procedures that were disrespectful of the rights of worthy recipients.

I felt that our welfare system was based on good intentions but did not provide dignifying opportunities for people on welfare to become employed. I felt that most recipients of public assistance would welcome employment in pursuits that could be of value to their communities while providing fair wages for persons who would otherwise require the assistance of public welfare.

Therefore, I proposed an alternative that would incorporate the helpful intentions of our welfare system by redefining the concept of work and encouraging local communities to employ their needy citizens in various new kinds of jobs.

The jobs would provide money from funds otherwise provided for traditional welfare programs under the sponsorship of public or private employers, for the performance of tasks of value to the community that were not menial in nature.

In other words, an elderly citizen might be employed as a "playground auntie" or "uncle," a gratifying role she or he could perform by observing and interacting with young children on the playground. Such a job would not be necessarily to babysit or supervise, but rather to be there to interact with the children, and would provide opportunities for interaction between the young and older citizens.

Another individual might operate a telephone reassurance program for shut-in citizens who were unable to communicate or relate to others in any other way. The notion of the program proposal was that local communities, often removed from the administration of public welfare, would be required to define work as any task determined to be of value to the local community and to offer at least some of our welfare recipients dignifying opportunities to make money and to avoid the negative aspects of public handouts.

How was this proposal to be funded? In working with an administrator from the state welfare office, we concluded that most, if not all, of the cost of such a program, could be borne from the same source of funds that supported public welfare. The proposal would have established a State Employment Board to which local communities would submit applications for local "jobs" programs.

By defining work as anything of value to the local community, the provisions of the legislation would have placed responsibility on local citizens for developing creative employment opportunities.

This idea was introduced quite late in the session, with little opportunity to be duly considered before the end of the session. I introduced the measure because I felt that we needed to generate alternatives to public welfare, and I hope that discussion of this measure might refine this idea or stimulate support for other alternatives. The bill was introduced and "left in the book" along with other introductory legislation.

Chapter 18
A Weighted-Vote Plan for Apportionment

Every ten years, state legislatures in the United States are required to reapportion the representative districts of the state to ensure, as near as feasible, that the concept of "one man – one vote" is realized.

This mandate means that at least every 10 years, state legislatures must determine a means to redraw and equitably balance the population size of the election districts of the state. During the fifty-sixth session of the Oregon legislature, the Republican party was the dominant party, so had the power (meaning enough votes) to determine the nature of the reapportionment plan for the state.

This meant that the power could, through careful manipulation, draw legislative boundaries in such a way as to work toward the election advantage of the Republican party. By knowing the makeup of each district, legislative district lines could be drawn to include a majority of voters from one party or another.

The problem I saw with this system of reapportionment was that, even if some semblance of equity could be found to satisfy both political parties, individual voters would still be disproportionately represented because of the variance of issue orientation expected to be found among any group of elected legislators.

In other words, in a close election, just over half (a constitutional majority) might well be represented by an economic-conservative legislator, while 49.99-percent of those casting votes may feel better represented by a more liberal legislator.

Therefore, I proposed a plan that would retain the traditional methods of reapportionment but continue after the election to provide each citizen-voter an opportunity to select which elected representative he wished to vote in his behalf on specific issues.

The plan would work in the following manner:

Following the election of all members of the state House of Representatives or state Senate, each voter would be provided a list of representatives and their stand on Pacific issues before the legislature.

Under usual circumstances, each elected representative would represent his constituency, casting one vote "yea" or "nay" on each issue or bill in the Senate or House of Representatives.

However, if any individual registered voter felt that his interests on a specific issue would be better represented by some representative or senator other than his locally elected official, he could choose to have the "weight" of his representation served by another legislator.

For example, if each member of the House of Representatives represented 35,000 voters, then each representative would have a one-vote weight of 35,000 in the state House of Representatives.

But any citizen voter who wished to have that legislator or any other represent him when voting on particular kinds of issues, could indicate his choice by filling out a mark-sensed card and mailing it to the state capital. This card would be validated and the intention of the voter processed.

The selected legislator, then, would cast votes for the citizen in the area of issue interest he had indicated. Thus, one legislator might cast a weighted vote on economic issues of considerably greater strength than the other legislator.

This system would provide the opportunity for any voter who feels strongly about a particular issue to have the individual legislator who most directly represents his point of view to do so. Further, it would encourage strong debate on issues, allowing individual citizens to express their attitudes and expectations in a manner that would allow for the will of the people to be heard. The weighted-vote plan would lessen several onerous aspects of our present system of representation politics.

Under the present system of representation, we have assumed that by redistricting the voter population, each voter would have exactly the same weight or representation in our state legislature. What actually happens is that the leadership selected by the majority party caucus holds supreme power, while the minority party members elected by the same number of voters hold very small amounts of power.

What is intended to be majority rule often results in rule by dictation of the party leadership of a majority of legislators in the dominant party caucus.
This arrangement allows far too much power to be wielded by an individual legislator who ideally represents the same number of voters as every other legislator. If this individual happens to represent a small, but powerful, minority faction in his or her part of the state, this legislator can hold other issues ransom to ensure that minority "pork barrel" issues are passed, sometimes before other more popularly supported ideas have a chance.

The present system further forces voters to select individual representatives who may represent their perspective on most of the issues, but do not represent them at all on others. Also, it may be difficult to know where the candidates stand on a particular issue until that issue emerges and is debated in the political arena.

The weighted-apportionment plan for voting would not ensure that the people of the state would be represented exactly in the same proportions as their attitudes on all issues. But, it would provide an option for aroused citizenry of voters to ensure that attention to the issues, rather than partisan politics and heavy imbalances of powerful minorities, controls the course of legislative decision making.

This idea was presented at a hearing before the Republican-dominated Elections Committee of the fifty-sixth legislative session in Oregon. It stimulated no discussion and no debate. The interest of the dominant party (and it would have been the same if the other party been dominant) was understandably pre-focused on rearranging the legislative districts of the state to encourage and ensure the election of their own party to succeeding sessions.

The outcome of this process of the fifty-sixth legislative session of Oregon was that the Republican party determined the new apportionment plan for the state and was able to effectively "pick-off" several members of the other party through implementation of their plan. I was one of those who were redistricted or placed in a single-member election district with a member of my own party (meaning that only one could be elected to the next session), and "bumped-off" at the next primary election.

By this gerrymandering of the legislative districts, I found myself cut off from my strongest constituency base and running for re-election in Springfield, Oregon, a city across the river from my residence. To have been re-elected would have meant moving to another district, perhaps across the street, or beating another incumbent who occupied the same voter territory.

By a creative redistricting plan, the Republican secretary of state (vested with the power to reapportion by the Republican-dominated legislature) could adjust the district lines at will. At one time, the district affecting me ran through the middle of my house and would have enabled me to run in a district with no incumbent by moving my bedroom from one end of the house to another.

It also allowed the secretary of state to inform me a few days before the final apportionment plan was announced, that I "had nothing to worry about." I was assured that the new apportionment plan would place me in a district with no incumbent.

Actually, when the new plan was announced, this was not the case. What this meant was a district of predominantly Republican votes was carved out of an area that would have otherwise been dominated by Democrats, ensuring the Republican party a sizable advantage in acquiring a Republican seat in the next session of the legislature while "bumping-off" a recently elected Democrat in the process.

That's politics!

Chapter 19
The "Humanitarian Award"

After the fifty-sixth legislative session was well under way, I received a telephone call and correspondence from a lawyer friend who represented several individuals who had an unusual problem. These persons had undergone operations to change their personal sexual identity. They had asked their lawyer, and in turn, me, to help change the law forbidding changes of sexual identity on driver's licenses.

The problem was that, although they had changed their physical anatomy and appearance to reflect their sexual choice, they were unable to change M (for male) or F (for female) on their license. Every time they were asked for identification, they had the problem of trying to explain the discrepancy between their appearance and the written information on the driver's license, the most common item of personal identification.

These individuals and their lawyers asked me to try to bring a change in the state law so the Records Department would allow such changes in identity to be reflected on official records. It didn't appear that this small change on a driver's license should be all that difficult, but I was to learn otherwise.

As usual procedure in preparing legislation, I submitted the information necessary for the legislative lawyers to draft the necessary proposal. The resulting bill appeared simple, but prior to the "Throwing it into the hopper," I checked with the Speaker of the House and asked that this sensitive bill be referred to an understanding committee with as little attention drawn to it as possible. I felt (and he agreed) that this bill had considerable potential for being misunderstood. I hoped that it could be introduced quietly, have a quiet hearing, (which is required on all proposed legislation before it is passed out of the committee) pass quietly through the senate and be signed into law.

This bill would affect, at that time, possibly six citizens in the state. But to them it was extremely important, and their legislature was the only means they had to effect changes in the law to allow personal identification information to be changed on driver's licenses.

The Speaker agreed to assign the bill to the committee that would understand the most about the legal implications of its contents, the House Judiciary Committee. I then "threw the bill into the hopper."

As usually happens, new legislation is pursued by the capitol press staff, and newspaper and television reports are made of all new bills introduced. Several members of the press corps contacted me about the "sex change" bill, and I could tell by their demeanor that the bill might have some difficulty in the press.

In each instance, I asked that they regard the bill seriously, as it was important to a few citizens and should not be highlighted particularly or used as the butt of jocularity. In all instances, they cooperated. Several small articles appeared, listing the proposed legislation along with other new bills introduced that day.

Next, I contacted the individuals who had asked me to introduce this legislation and asked them to prepare testimony for the House Judiciary Committee. The head of the Judiciary Committee cooperated with my request to schedule a quiet hearing for the bill and assigned it to a very late evening hearing.

This cooperation could not, however, squelch the jokes, sophomoric statements, and supposed good-natured ribbing I was to encounter. The hearing in the House Judiciary Committee went quietly enough, with only one person appearing to be in opposition to the legislation. This lady was in charge of the state records, and her testimony was officious, pert, and brief. The testimony in favor of the legislation was carefully worded to explain the importance of this bill to a few people and to encourage its passage without undue discussion.

Unfortunately, several of the lawyers on the Judiciary Committee did not understand the difference between transsexual and transvestite, and other terms all seemed charged with great humor. The entire hearing was marked by a controlled undercurrent of mirth, with knowing glances and smirks exchanged between committee members. I tried as best I could in my own testimony to answer questions and encourage serious consideration of this bill. As this was the first hearing for this legislation, no decision was made during the hearing and further consideration of the matter was to be made at a later date.

As the legislature approached adjournment, I could not get this bill to a second hearing in the committee, and it was finally "left at the table" at the conclusion of the session. Some individual members of the Judiciary Committee, I understood, were not willing to have a positive vote recorded on this legislation and subsequently reported to their constituents. Such a vote, to at least several of them, would have meant possible ridicule and embarrassment.

To me, it brought neither but developed in me considerable anger and disrespect for my insensitive colleagues on the Judiciary Committee. I know that brief piece of legislation was handled as well as I could have guided it under the circumstances.

It was a sad commentary on the legal professionalism of the lawyers on the committee, several of whom would probably become judges in the state, that a small change affecting only a few people, and which had to be made by the legislature alone, could not be processed. The citizens would either have to go to court or continue their battle in subsequent legislatures. Nor was the lack of action by the Judiciary Committee the end of the issue for me.

Following the adjournment of the fifty-sixth session of the legislature, both the Senate and House members assembled in the House chambers for presentation of awards to members of both houses who had performed in particularly noteworthy fashion during the session and deserved acclaim of their legislative colleagues.

These awards, called "turkey awards," were intended to provide joviality and to help mend the political wounds and egos produced by the political machinations of the session. With much hilarity, several of my colleagues and myself received awards.

With much laughter and thigh slapping, I was called to the rostrum, and under the blaze of television cameras and the mirthful eyes of my colleagues, I was awarded the "Humanitarian Award" for the session, a cold and greasy (but huge) cooked turkey leg.

I was very angry and was afraid the tears that I felt in my eyes would give away my emotion. I considered refusing the award but had to do something quickly. I composed myself, walked as briskly and as straight as my six-foot-four-inch frame could portray, and with as much seriousness and dignity as I could muster accepted the greasy turkey leg, hoping that my appearance might pique the conscience of at least some of my political friends.

I didn't mind being called the "humanitarian" of the session, but to at least six rightful citizens of the state of Oregon, and myself, I had failed.

Chapter 20
A Bill for Hitchers, Hikers, and Bikers

Shortly after the beginning of the legislative session, a constituent contacted me regarding a bill introduced by the Transportation Committee at the instigation of the state police. This bill, if enacted, would eliminate all hitchhiking on state highways. The constituent was concerned that if this legislation passed, people could not hitchhike, and for many people, this would not only be a hardship, but would necessitate owning cars, becoming more environmentally unconscious, and would represent another small infringement on individual rights.

I recognized the fear of hitchhikers held by some people but had never felt that anyone had to pick up hitchhikes if they didn't want to. Also, I had an idea in mind that would make "ride sharing" safe.

By introducing a positive alternative to eliminating hitchhiking, I felt there might be some opportunity to establish a ride-sharing system and asked the Legislative Council to prepare a bill that would create transportation alternatives for people who wished to walk, or ride bikes or horses, rather than depend on the automobile as the sole source of transportation on public highways. My strategy was to get the Transportation Committee to table the anti-hitchhiking bill, then I would submit a positive alternative that might have some chance of passage.

Before the date of the hearing in the Transportation Committee regarding the anti-hitchhiking bill, I received a visit from a college student who represented several thousand students who had signed petitions against the hitchhiking bill. This group asked me to represent their interest in the legislative hearing and present the petitions to the Transportation Committee.

I explained that I would be happy to talk on their behalf, as I agreed with their approach, but suggested that they represent themselves and in sizable numbers at the hearing. I began to receive considerable mail on the issue, and one constituent mentioned an older lady who was known as the "hitchhiking grandma." Through volunteers, I was able to contact her, and she agreed to present testimony against the hitchhiking measure.

It is always a particularly interesting hearing when hundreds of citizens attend, all wishing to make their voice heard. And it was my experience that it was much easier to get people to attend hearings when they were against something than for it. As I had been promised, several hundred people of all ages attended, who had signed petitions against the proposal earlier.I testified early in the hearing, as is the deference extended to elected officials.

The most interesting testimony by far was that presented by the "hitchhiking grandma." She related interesting stories about her experiences hitchhiking thousands of miles to visit her grandchildren, sometimes enjoying police escort from one edge of town to the other, and even sleeping in a jail one night at the suggestion of a supportive policeman.

Hitchhiking had allowed her to travel extensively at virtually no cost. It was difficult for legislators to be against the little old lady, and the measure was tabled after considerable discussion. Had this hearing not been held, I believe it is quite possible that the Oregon legislature would have followed the example of other states and outlawed hitchhiking.

My "hitchers, hikers and bikers" bill, though well received, didn't get through the legislature, either. I was, however, a sponsor of another bill that did. A Republican colleague had asked me to sign with him on a bill that enjoyed the support of a sizable number of representatives and senators. Under this legislation, Oregon became the first state to require that a percentage of highway funds be dedicated to building bike paths. This example has been followed by most states since and is a required regulation in some highway fund expenditures of the federal government.

Chapter 21
A Proposal for Fair Qualifications for Employment

Part of the advantage of working on someone's campaign is the payoff in having them work directly for you after the election. One such instance was a constituent who had worked on my campaign knowing we had similar philosophical commitments and that I could be called upon to introduce legislation of particular interest to him. It is no problem for any legislator to have a bill drafted and to introduce it. But in this instance, I agreed heartily with this citizen's suggestion.

Too often, he explained, persons are denied employment because they do not possess certain qualifications, even though they could perform the job adequately. Too often, educational qualifications unrelated to the performance of a particular job are used to include and exclude applicants.

Otherwise, well-prepared individuals are considered unqualified because they lack a particular educational certificate or degree, the preparation for which have little or nothing to do with the ability of the applicant to perform the job for which he or she has applied.

To correct this injustice, I had a bill drafted that would make it unlawful for the state of Oregon to include in job applications, requirements unrelated to the applicant's ability to adequately perform the job.

As an educator, I was aware that this particular bill, if passed, would have serious repercussions in the professional education community. As in other professions requiring degrees and certificates, having the necessary qualifications for applying for teaching jobs does not necessarily mean that the certified person is really capable of teaching well.

At the same time, individuals who possess unusually high skills and might make fine instructors are sometimes denied suitable teaching assignments because they lack required certification. The point of the proposed legislation was that unless degrees or certificates are meaningfully related to specific job qualifications, these requirements could not be used as a test for employment in that job.

This proposal met welcome approval from labor unions and from the state director of employment, a former state senator. The state superintendent of public instruction agreed to testify on behalf of the bill (as the former two individual did) but on the day of the hearing, did not show up. I suspect the implications for the field of education made the state superintendent's absence wise.

Before this bill was heard by the State and Federal Affairs Committee, the constituent who had suggested the legislation had another interesting idea. He suggested that we might add a financial penalty to the bill as follows:

An employer requiring an irrelevant educational degree would be penalized one-thirtieth of the cost to the state in supporting the preparation of one graduate with that degree. In other words, an employer could require a Ph.D. for a building maintenance repair person, but unless he could prove that the degree had specific job-related relevance, the employer could be fined one-thirtieth the cost per year that the state incurred in helping prepare a Ph.D. for graduation.

Or if an employer required a high school diploma for a person to be hired as a janitor (an actual case), the employer could be taken to court and assessed fines commensurate with the cost of the state for preparing a high school student for graduation.

Although this was an interesting bill, it presented considerable difficulty in defining relevance of tasks required in many jobs and might have been extremely difficult to implement.

Since that time, similar legislation and regulations have been originated at the state level as a result of court cases involving equity in hiring. Like many ideas presented to the legislatures all over the country, they usually pass only when the public is ready for them and seldom because of the altruistic interests of legislators.

Chapter 22
After the Session and Before the Next Election

By the end of a lengthy session (about six months), the ninety members of the Oregon legislature returned to their homes knowing that a special or interim session on finance would probably be necessary. Most editorials heralded by the fifty-sixth legislative session in Oregon as "one of the best in history." It was characterized by (for its time) legislation, such as the first "bottle bill," which required a deposit on certain cans and bottles, a revised juvenile code for the state, a ban on field burning in agriculture, and hundreds of other pieces of legislation, most of which had little interest to most citizens but were important as housekeeping matters necessary for state operation.

When asked to comment on the effectiveness and satisfaction than most. I felt that the session was characterized more by what it had failed to do than by what it had accomplished.

None of the major proposals that I had introduced were passed into law. This was not unusual, as freshman legislators in minority parties seldom are successful initiators of new legislation.

Many bills, however, on which the new representative shared sponsorship with others did pass. Often, legislative measures must be introduced several times before sufficient success to pass all legislative hurdles. Much of the success that elected officials might claim for themselves is never visible to the public.

As an opposite example, the Camp Adair issue was highly visible and was accomplished as well as I might have hoped it could, even though the memorial, which made the issue a legislative matter, died in committee. At the same time, I was the sponsor (along with many others) on the bottle bill and the bike bill, both issues that might have originated, but issues that probably would not have succeeded without the major sponsorship of other, more powerful, legislators affiliated with the "in" party.

An issue to require taxation of church property, and that reflected heavy separation of church and state consideration, was sponsored by a Republican colleague who was joined by me and others. This measure received a lot of attention and much healthy testimony but was defeated. This and similar issues, had been proposed at several earlier sessions of the legislature. The representative who proposed the bill to require taxation of church property was also a major Republican sponsor of the state bike bill, and was successful along with other "signed on" sponsors, including me.

The end of the fifty-sixth legislative session really marked the beginning of the next session, and all legislators returned home to begin the long and hard campaign on behalf of issues they had "left on the table" and their own re-election campaigns.

For my family, the first task following the legislative session was to move back home and put the family pieces back together again, including my employment.

Oregon legislators at that time were paid $250 per month during the interim between sessions, hardly enough to support their families. Some legislators would be involved in interim committees, but these assignments usually went to majority party members or senior legislators, but with only per diem expenses paid in addition to the meager monthly salary.

For those legislators not released from continuing contracts, job hunting was a necessity. In my case, this meant seeking employment with the knowledge that I would soon have to be campaigning again if I chose to run for re-election, a prospect not too attractive to most educational employers. For schoolteachers on continuing contracts, leaves of absence were possible. In my case, I had to find work that could be terminated or delayed in keeping with my dominant legislative schedule. This I was able to do by piecing together some college teaching and some consulting work, leaving the question of re-election plans open for the time being.

Once home from the legislature, I found my work as a legislator continued. The "Call LeRoy" phone continued to be a source of information for interested constituents and a means for me to maintain contact with the citizens I represented. Actually, there was less than one year remaining before my own re-election plans would have to be finalized. I found that being a state representative was like being a continual candidate. I was often asked to speak at meetings and as an incumbent legislator, was expected to know far more than I did during my campaign.

The six months in the legislature had been a fantastic experience and training opportunity, both for citizenship as well as for my continued political life. I was quite sure I would want to run for office again but also very sure that the issues that motivated my participation in politics would have to take precedence over my own electability.

The following pages relate some of the issues in which I became involved, some of which others felt may have helped end my brief political career.

Chapter 23
Public Ownership of Land

I am really not sure what motivates some people, myself included, to take on issues that are wrought with potentially disastrous consequences, but nonetheless require advocacy. Such a controversial issue was a proposal I made to the Lane County Democratic Party Platform Convention.

If any of my political followers had reason to doubt my sanity in the past, this issue turned their doubts into assurance.

I guess I always believed that the so-called "God-given" substances such as air, water and sunlight belong to all of us equally, and that no one has a right to destroy them, as the future livelihood and sustenance of all of us depend on these "commons."

As I grew in my understanding of environmental concerns, I came to realize that other substances besides air, water and sunlight deserved the same consideration. As I studied the problem of ecological balance and the importance to humankind of strict adherence to basic principles that seemed inherent in the interaction of these environmental realities, I could not separate the earth, or land, from other natural gifts.

I had no quarrel with temporary ownership, as long as that ownership was accompanied with adequate responsibility to ensure that future generations would have a livable total environment for sustenance and happiness that past generations had inherited.

It was during the Lane County Democratic Platform Convention that I decided I must propose the concept of land as a common heritage and a part of our ecological support system worthy of the protection of all of us. I hastily scratched a proposal on the back of an envelope and to the consternation of some and the delight of others was able to convince the county representatives of the Democratic party that such an idea or "plank" belonged in the county platform.

I proposed the notion because I felt that debate of such an important issue needed to be started and that such an idea would certainly encourage citizens of the county to read and debate the contents of the Democratic platform.

The adamant protest by the majority voting against this platform proposal and the treatment it was to receive throughout the coming campaign proved me to be right. I had wanted debate of the platform planks. The public ownership of land proposal assured most Democratic candidates of more debate and association with the Democratic party platform than they wanted.

What I proposed was that individuals or groups be allowed to obtain temporary title to land property, only if such land was used in a way that it was preserved, protected, and enhanced in ways that would continue to keep it as a valuable common resource and part of the ecological heritage of future generations. I did not argue with the concept of temporary ownership. I felt this was essentially what contemporary ownership of land already encompassed.

Didn't the state already grant ownership under specific state restrictions? Had anyone ever maintained ownership of land to themselves after they died? What I was really interested in, was that land be recognized as a common environmental substance and deserving of the common ownership and care by all of us.

This issue certainly got the attention, as I had hoped it would, of the Lane County Democrats and the news media as well. Suddenly, I found myself called all kinds of interesting names. One group even seriously considered taking up a collection to "send me back to Russia" (Soviet Union). When this was related to me, I wondered how my Nebraska farmer-rancher forebears would have taken this information.

I was challenged to several exciting debates, notably one with the Washington County, Oregon Board of

Realtors, near Portland. This group had asked me to address one of their periodic "in-service" sessions (continued in-service training of realtors was a requirement of state law).

My wife accompanied me on this occasion and we enjoyed a rather fine banquet dinner prior to my presentation. I was not a candidate in this area, but the issue was of such terrifying audaciousness that they could hardly ignore me.

During my presentation, I quoted a beautiful and almost poetic description of what this issue was all about from a book called *Crosscreek*, authored by Marjorie Kinnan Rawlings, who had also written the American children's classic *The Yearling*.

At the end of my speech, an inebriated realtor swayed to her feet and nastily demanded, "Who is that communist you quoted?" I was delighted that the chairman recognized the name of the author I had quoted and informed his professional associate with no help from me.

I found no support for the idea that land, like air, water and sunlight, is a part of the common support system for all living things. The notion that present ownership practices are, in effect, already a form of temporary ownership was not accepted. The emotional feelings raised by this issue transcended its rational consideration. I didn't really expect a group of real estate dealers to feel otherwise.

If this idea was such an anathema to the people of Oregon, and to the Democratic party particularly, why was it accepted by a majority of representative Democrats at both the county level, (Land County) and at the state Democratic Party Convention, held in Klamath Falls, Oregon, that year?

I think that issue made inherent sense to almost everyone, but at the same time it ran directly into the desire of practically every citizen to own a piece of land, to cultivate it, and to set one's roots in the permanence of the soil. I share that feeling and take some satisfaction in the huge body of law and precedent that is being developed to ensure that land and its resources, like sunlight, air, and water, require continued responsibility of all of us to insure the continued usability for future generations.

As I debated this issue, I tried to redirect attention to immediate concerns of Oregon citizens and my immediate constituents in the newly formed representative district in which I found myself a candidate for re-election. I think I must have been the only Democrat in the state who had not "jumped off the platform" during that election campaign.

If another issue, even more rambunctious than the concept of private ownership of land, and which I had also been successful in getting into the state Democratic platform, had been understood, I would have experienced even more vehement opposition. I had proposed an amendment to the U.S. Constitution that, if finally approved, would have mandated the concept of "original responsibility" in all actions endangering environmental security of all our commonly owned resources.

Chapter 24
A Proposal for a Legal Concept of "Original Responsibility"

What was really behind the concept of public ownership of land was the notion of responsibility. Altruistically, all persons ought to be responsible in their actions toward their environment, including the way they treat the physical resources they need for survival and how they relate to other human beings and living things.

All are related passengers on the spaceship earth.

I felt our traditional way of ensuring responsibility was negative. Rather than tell people what they shouldn't do, I felt it would be a great improvement in our concept of public responsibility to require that individuals and groups behave in such a way toward one another and their environment, that they accept "original responsibility" for their actions. By this, I meant that no one should knowingly take action that is detrimental to the "commons," or the resources that all living entities require to sustain themselves ecologically.

Conceptionally, this meant that a person or a group should be liable for damage done to the commons, unless the public specifically agreed that a trade-off of damage to our common resources was outweighed by the public good derived from that damage. Thus, if the production or transference of energy (from one energy source to a usable form) was recognized to be in the public good, then damage to the environment to originate or transfer that energy would be an acceptable trade-off.

Important to this notion is that all persons be responsible as citizens to make choices. No individual or group, without the approval of society, could make such decisions, or they would (or could) be held "originally responsible" and could be required to make amends. An action subsequently found to have detrimental environment effects upon the common resources of society would make the perpetrator of the act liable to replace or return the resource to its former condition. This notion was not intended to stop "progress," but rather to encourage and require responsibility for actions taken by those who would reap personal gain at the expense of future inheritance and sustenance of the rest of us.

I had hoped that the concept of "original responsibility" would receive much debate, but it didn't. And as our law continues to operate, we blindly accept the proposition of "environment aware" and allow anything to be done to our common resources that is not strictly forbidden by law. We continue to legally list the "can'ts" and "don'ts" while the payoff to develop common resources goes to those who can mine or develop the resources prior to government control or intervention.

I felt strongly that the cost of maintaining or sustaining our environment should be borne by those of us who use the resources, and the cost should be built into the purchase price. The concept of "original responsibility" requires the cost to society be considered before action is taken and when the public decides it must develop and use a common resource that is irreplaceable or difficult to replace. At the same time, it agrees to pay the cost of losing the future use of the resource or to pay for its renewal.

CHAPTER 25
CITIZEN POLITICS NOW AND LATER

The events related in this book have been presented from my subjective perspective. Since that experience, I attempted an additional (unsuccessful) foray into politics by running for a nonpartisan position as state superintendent of public instruction in Oregon. Subsequent professional work in American Samoa and the state of Alaska enabled me to reminisce about citizen politics from a somewhat more objective vantage point than would have been earlier possible.

Looking back, I often wonder what did I find to be particularly valuable about my brief encounter with political machinations? What effect did that experience have on my family as well as my own political outlook?

Even though these remarks were written about events that happened over 10 years ago, it has been difficult for me to think objectively about them. Perhaps it never will be. However, I think it valuable to review one's attitudes and feelings in order to be a more effective participant in future endeavors and a more accurate observer of future happenings.

Looking back, I am pleased that I sought political office and was provided with the opportunity to attempt to translate personal ideas into political action. In 1970, the year of my first political venture, I am sure I felt much the same frustration that other citizens felt who had been active participants in the fervent quest for change in the 1960s. I felt much frustration during the presidential election of 1968 when millions of Americans vicariously shared the violent experience of the so-called "Chicago riots" during the national Democratic party convention. I agonized greatly as I observed individuals who seemed to have had ideals similar to mine get their heads bashed in on the streets of Chicago as they protested being shut out of the very political process that many felt provided the best hope for political change. Senator Eugene McCarthy had somehow appealed to the ideals of many Americans in that political primary, and the Democratic party rules and the manipulation of those rules by powerful vested interests in the power structure of the Democratic party left these activists with little more than frustration. Many of them had tried to be active and orderly participants, working through the traditional political system, only to find themselves rejected by party rules written by and for those who wish to hold power for themselves.

This frustration finally erupted in the streets and demonstrated to all Americans the ugly crack in our democratic idealism. Our political system was supposed to provide all citizens with equal access to political power, and the Chicago convention of 1968 demonstrated that even the more open of our political parties, the national Democratic party, and the party rules controlling the process for nomination of presidential candidates were written to provide unequal power to the party bosses.

During my initial attempt to be elected to political office in 1970, the hurt of the 1968 Chicago convention was so much in the minds and hearts of the members of the Democratic party, especially the younger people. Many had lost hope in the potential of the American political system for bringing change and had withdrawn. At the same time, disenchantment with attempts to bring the Vietnam War to a close added higher octane to the fuel of frustration with out "establishment," which, rather than lose power and influence, employed representative power to maintain order. Many of us awakened to find the "establishment" to be us, and our inattention to the important political issues of the time supported the refusal of our system to right itself.

It is only fair to recognize that not all Americans shared the same perspective on these events of the 1960s. The "Chicago riots" demonstrated the use of police force to quell what many perceived to be intolerable and uncalled-for uprisings. Also, it became clear later that all participants in the "riots" were not idealistic Democrats. Nor was it clear that the actions of the police were entirely reactionary and necessary to preserve order.

It later was ascertained that, in some instances, the police provoked tension and violence rather than reduced it. What seemed to have happened in the streets of Chicago was a release of two conflicting tensions. Many Americans were calling for a more open political system through which grievances could be addressed, and other Americans, at the same time, perceived the issues of political stress and anti-Vietnam feeling and related activities to be intolerable challenges to our country.

In 1970, the intensity of these two issues continued, and some of the veterans of the 1968 confrontations, directly and vicariously, had decided to become active participants in party politics. My campaign provided the means for participation that some of these citizens, including me, needed. Although I had not participated in the activities of 1968, like many Americans of that era, I had become increasingly frustrated with the immobility and inaccessibility of the American political system and had worked with groups who did not understand that system well and were frustrated with what was happening locally and nationally. Many citizens felt that they were powerless within their own government and, rather than face frustration of continuing defeat, withdrew from the fray and vented their frustration. This provided in a minimal way for some idealistic participation and an attempt to bring about change.

The Citizen Participation Committee of the Owens campaign provided a direct opportunity to participate in change in a variety of ways. The idea of citizen participation really utilized the theory of Cognitive Dissonance that I had employed in my work as a teacher trainer and project director with older people. As related early in this book, this theory states that if individuals are aware that things are not as they wish them to be (Cognitive Dissonance) and they are provided an acceptable alternative that is potentially satisfying and obtainable, they will seek the alternative.

In this instance, I provided, as a candidate, an acceptable alternative to "politics as usual." My candidacy allowed some of my supporters an opportunity to bring about acceptable change without threatening the security of the on-going political system. Several young supporters cut their long hair to become more effective campaigners in their interaction with citizens who were challenged by male individuals who wore their hair down to their shoulders and seemed to visually identify with "radicals."

Some supporters could be "somebody" by interacting with people of various backgrounds in the common effort to elect an acceptable candidate to public office. Even though I spoke in somewhat radical ways, I wore a business suit and closely cropped hair, and was, as I had been in the past, employed in entirely acceptable pursuits.

Thus, my election efforts offered a low-risk, low-cost alternative opportunity for involvement and the potential for bringing about political change. To a large number of supporters, a candidate represented their own ideals, and his election could result in their own vicarious and representative participation more directly in their own political system.

My work with older Americans in the late 1960s had convinced me that the same frustrations felt by many younger people were shared by older citizens as well. My own frustrations with our political system did not vary a great deal from what either group seemed to exemplify. This political alienation was not different than the reaction of the people of any age to institutions they were expected to support. These institutions seemed, however, to increasingly represent attitudes and take actions alien to the personal expectations of the people.

As a consultant for the National Council on Aging (NCOA), I was asked to work with numerous groups of older Americans in different states.

Among all these groups, I observed a similar alienation. Many of these people expressed they had little positive relationship to their own government. Most of them had never participated actively in the decision-making process that resulted in decisions affecting their lives. Most had a "textbook" feeling about American politics but had never actively participated in bringing change. They felt unrelated to those who did.

When given the opportunity to participate in helping to determine the direction of decision making that affected them specifically, and especially when they felt even some small degree of success, the citizens became "turned-on" and "hooked" by their own political system. When they were able to see inside the system and to become effective participants in that system, many became active in the same way that was exemplified in our campaign.

Individuals who had characterized politics as being "dirty," came to see politics rather as a reflection of a condition of American society. I came to see my responsibility as a candidate to provide avenues for involvement from a wide range of citizen perspectives, as a means to collecting support for my own campaign.

I came to realize that many people were not supporting me as much as they were supporting their own dedication to ideals and issues. I was the means through which they could identify with their own political system. My campaign became an acceptable alternative to the frustration and anger (Cognitive

Dissonance) that they recognized. And I developed an appreciation for the political power of aggressive citizen politics.

"But how," the reader may ask, "did the author see his own participation in politics?" As a candidate and later as an elected state representative, I came to view our American political system as one entirely based upon the continuing perspective of our voting citizenry. I, like too many Americans, possessed a "textbook" misperception about our political system. I found most politicians, at local, state, and national levels, to be earnest and dedicated individuals. Most elected officials, I found, had pet interests and often held viewpoints alien to my own. Seldom, however, did I find these perspectives to be hidden and dishonest. I found most politicians to be personable and the kind of people you would enjoy having as next-door neighbors. I found the Oregon House of Representatives and Senate to be a very direct portrayal of the perspectives and idiosyncrasies of the citizens of the state of Oregon.

I admit I did not always enjoy that reality, but I came to remind myself often that each representative was elected by a community of approximately 33,000 citizens. I could be critical (and often was) of the stances of my colleagues, but I came to realize that they were entitled to their opinions just as much as I was to mine.

In one instance, I was visited by a constituency of citizens from a rural district who felt they were not well represented by their elected representative. I was a member of the Agriculture Committee, and they hoped I could help them gain support for their perspective on a particular bill. I found myself helping to educate them on how to become more politically effective and suggested ways they might influence other legislators to appreciate their viewpoint.

Following my advice, these farmers contacted specific representatives by night letter and the following day were effective in swinging an expected negative vote in the direction they wished it to go. Without their acceptance of responsibility to educate their elected representatives, and those from other districts as well, they would have not received the favorable vote they sought.

Increasingly, I found my role as an elected representative as one of providing leadership for educating my constituency to the issues at hand and directing their expression of citizen responsibility in influencing other representatives to vote with me, or me with them, on particular issues. As a freshman minority party leader, I held very little political power or influence. I found that I had to somehow influence others with my own power of persuasion behind the scenes, which proved extremely valuable.

Although I was effective on some issues such as Camp Adair, the real power of the legislature rested with those who were elected by their majority party to exercise process power and could control the entire flow of legislation, manipulating the votes of many legislators through their control of the political machinery. I came to appreciate the power of party politics for good as well as bad. I began to see that electing a majority of Democrats to both the House and Senate in the next elections was of prime importance, if any of the ideas I wished to propose in legislation were to have any chance of passage. I became convinced that a majority of like-interested candidates had to be elected in order for political change to occur.

This meant at least a cadre of interested citizens would have to form behind each of these candidates and build a political base that could ultimately be expressed in future legislative votes on public issues.

My experience in being elected and in serving, taught me that political power can be amassed by a few and exercised to the advantage of a few, only when the voting public allows this to happen.

Since my brief experience in elected politics, several changes have been made to encourage a more open political process. Public disclosure of individual wealth and the source of campaign funds has provided voters with improved tools for making election decisions.

Better campaign financing requirements tend to equalize access to political office a bit more for the less-wealthy candidates than their well-heeled opponents. But none of these changes replaced the necessity of a dedicated and responsible voting public.

My experience in the Oregon legislature reinforced my notion that people get the kind of government they deserve. If politicians are representative of the general public in their attitudes and expectations, and if those of the public are generally low, then we can expect a government imbued with the machinations of power politics with the interests of our society generally manipulated to the advantage of a few.

If we strive to have a government based on a well-informed electorate, behaving responsibly to elect officials to represent their well-informed viewpoint, then political decisions will be made by well-informed legislators in the best interest of the public generally. If elected officials perceive their role, as I did, to keep the constituencies well informed and to lead the debate on the major issues of the time, then politics can become the means through which society adjusts and renews itself to the continued betterment of its people.

There are no guarantees in a democracy that we will always make the right decisions, elect the right representatives, and determine always the best solutions. The strength of democracy, finally, is its flexibility while maintaining the basic rights and processes for governmental self-renewal.

Believing this, after my term in the Oregon legislature, I began to teach classes in practical politics, continuing to do so beyond my term of office. I have had the satisfaction of seeing several students successfully campaign and come to hold positions in local and state government. None of these individuals totally agreed with me on all issues, nor was it important that they should have. My only hope is that they and more citizens recognize and continue to recognize that our political system provides the means for resolving the issues of our times and for continually improving the human condition. It is the responsibility of all citizens to do what they can to ensure that we continue to have an ever better-informed public that strives to always elect individuals who will serve in the best interest of all. We can only trust our own exercise of responsibility.

I intended, in writing this book, to relate the experience of one citizen-politician in the hope that each reader might be stimulated, and some motivated, to participate more directly in elective government. The issues that I have related may or may not have particular importance in themselves. I have related discussion of them in a desire to continue to stimulate debate and the formation of well-informed opinion. I will enjoy talking about these ideas and hope that I will someday see portions of them adopted. I am not sure that by the time this may come about, my own views will not be considerably different from those expressed in this writing.

In the meantime, reader, it is important for you and me to inform ourselves better and demand that those we choose to support and elect do likewise – for, finally, government will be as good as we make it and as inventive and rewarding as our expectations demand.

ABOUT THE AUTHOR

Dr. LeRoy D. Owens

Dr. LeRoy Owens was born on March 7, 1934, in Harrison, Nebraska. He holds a master's degree in school administration from the University of Idaho and a doctorate in education from the University of Oregon. At the time of this writing Dr. Owens and his wife, Mary Jo, resided in Dillingham, Alaska, where he was superintendent of schools for the Dillingham City School System. They retired actively in Ashland, Oregon.

Find out more at **amazon.com/author/leroyowens**

CAN I ASK A FAVOR?

If you enjoyed this book, found it useful or otherwise, then I'd really appreciate it if you would post a short review on Amazon. I do read all the reviews personally so I can continue to write, respond and stay relevant. Thanks for your support!

BOOK NOTES

Memoirs of a Citizen-Politician is the reflection of an honest, idealistic man who ran on the Democratic ticket for the Oregon House of Representatives in 1970 and, after all is said and done, came out a winner.

LeRoy Owens served only one term in the Oregon state legislature, yet he gained priceless insight into the workings of the democratic process and came away with the belief that people get the kind of government they deserve. This book shares those insights, the joy and disappointments of public responsibility.

Dr. Owens's candid appraisal of our political system will inspire even the most apathetic citizen to take a more serious look at his role in local, state, and federal government. Memoirs of a Citizen-Politician is a positive, uplifting statement that is a must read for every American.